# my favourite
# restaurants
## Calgary, Canmore and beyond

eighth edition

# John Gilchrist
### edited by Catherine Caldwell

Escurial Incorporated
Calgary, Alberta

Published by
Escurial Incorporated
9519 Assiniboine Road SE
Calgary, Alberta, Canada T2J 0Z5
Phone: 403.255.7560
Email: escurial@telus.net

**Library and Archives Canada Cataloguing in Publication**

Gilchrist, John, 1953–, author
    My favourite restaurants : Calgary, Canmore and beyond /
John Gilchrist ; edited by Catherine Caldwell. — 8th edition.

Includes index.
Previous title: My favourite restaurants : Calgary, Banff and beyond,
© 2009.

ISBN 978–0–9868584–1–3 (pbk.)

    1. Restaurants—Alberta—Calgary—Guidebooks.
2. Restaurants—Alberta—Canmore—Guidebooks. 3. Restaurants—Alberta—Guidebooks. I. Caldwell, Catherine, 1956–, editor II. Title.

TX910.C2G54 2013        647.957123'38        C2013–904831–6

Credits:
Interior Design: Jeremy Drought, Last Impression Publishing Service,
    Calgary, Alberta
Cover Design: Pierre Lamielle, Calgary, Alberta
Printed and bound in Canada by Friesens Corporation, Altona, Manitoba

# Contents

# Acknowledgements

**T**HE first accolade in this book goes to the charming Catherine Caldwell, my wife and editor. I am blessed with having a world-class editor as a partner—without her, my books would simply not exist. She's a world-champion porridge maker (really) and can solve all the stylistic and grammatical conundrums that drive me batty (sometimes while stirring Highwood Crossing oats at the same time).

And here's a shout-out to our families and to Barb and Bob Gerst, Richard and Brenda White, and Karen Vavra, all of whom have helped in different ways through the all-consuming process of birthing a new book.

I also want to thank our two designers. There's Jeremy Drought, who created the interior of the book. He seems to know what we need even before we know we need it, and he pays attention to the minutest details, for which we are so very grateful. And there's Pierre Lamielle, who designed the front cover. He has a flare for creativity and a stunning knowledge of computer illustration.

A tip of my hat goes to Harry Sanders, whose book *Historic Walks of Calgary* has added depth to my knowledge of various restaurant locations. In a similar vein, thanks to historian David Finch, whose encyclopedic knowledge of Southern Alberta's stories has also been a real asset. And a big hug goes to Shelley Youngblut for saying nice things about me in the Foreword.

I don't want to forget the Calgary Downtown Association and two great people there—Maggie Schofield and Caralyn Macdonald. They've provided the map for all the downtown locations (49!) in this book.

And finally, a big thank you to all the chefs, servers, restaurateurs and food producers who make dining in Southern Alberta so interesting. That includes a caffeinated high-five to Shawn McDonald who fuels us with his fine Paradise Mountain coffees, especially the Angel's espresso.

# Foreword by Shelley Youngblut

I'VE eaten out in Calgary most of my life, yet whenever I make a reservation at a new hot spot, walk into an old favourite or discover a potential hidden gem, I still pause before committing to eat there and ask myself, "But what does John think of Restaurant X?"

We've got this relationship, you see, built on 33 years of his reviewing restaurants in the *Calgary Herald* and on CBC Radio's *Calgary Eyeopener*. I trust him. I believe him. I want to have what he's having.

With so many options out there, we're hungry to know what John knows, which is pretty much everything about the people and spaces that make up the dining-out landscape in Calgary, Canmore and beyond. He's interviewed all the chefs and restaurateurs, poured over cookbooks and history books, gone to the ends of the earth to sample ethnic food at the source, and eaten hundreds, no thousands, of meals.

Does that make John an expert? Absolutely. We shouldn't expect anything less from a restaurant critic. But as a sign of true Western hospitality, he sees himself as our personal host with the inside goods, which he generously divulges in these pages. He won't steer you wrong, and there might be more than a few delicious surprises.

Mind you, he's old school, albeit with an adventurous mind. (That's why there are 155 new entries in this 8th edition.) John says he's part of a dying breed: the professional, in-depth critic. Great reviews, like good food, take time to prepare and deserve to be savoured. What he knows can't be distilled into a 140-character tweet and what he sees can't be captured on Instagram. He checks out most places more than once, but never on opening night when it's more about sizzle than substance. He notes the service and the ambience, zeroing in on how it feels to be in a room. He's seen it all, eaten it all, as Calgary cuisine continues to combine ambitious cooking with entrepreneurial brashness.

"Don't tell me about the food," John says to young writers who want to follow in his size-eight footsteps. "That's the obvious thing."

No, what John is after is something more soulful—a truly satisfying dining experience. And he's the guy who knows where to find it.

*Shelley Youngblut was the founding editor of* Swerve, *Calgary's award-winning weekly magazine, and is a frequent contributor to CBC Radio's* Calgary Eyeopener. *One of the founding editors of* ESPN the Magazine, *she believes John Gilchrist is the Gordie Howe of restaurant critics.*

# Introduction

**N**UMBER Eight. It's been four years since Number Seven, and there have been huge changes in the Calgary dining scene. Some places have passed on, but many more have risen up to replace them. It's been a prolific time. Calgary is now widely considered to have one of the hottest and most interesting food cultures in North America. There's a huge amount of talent here.

The 2008 recession helped redefine how we eat out: Like everywhere across North America, we're not so much into fancy these days. Not to say we've gone sweatpants sloppy, but we are definitely more informal. At the same time, though, we've become more demanding of quality, value, variety, service and all-round positive dining experiences.

And the local restaurant scene has been happy to accommodate. We've seen creative ideas flourish—from tapas and vegetarian-Thai to contemporary doughnuts and gluten-free fare. We've embraced craft beer, third-wave coffee, artisanal ice cream, corkage and hyperlocal cuisine, all of which you'll find in this book. And we've gone gaga over food trucks, with over 40 now on the streets. I've included some of my favourites here, but for more info (including where they're parked), check out **streetfoodapp.com/Calgary** and **yycfoodtrucks.com**. Perhaps oddly, I've also included several restaurants that weren't yet open when we went to press, but were slated to open soon. Based on the track records of the chefs/owners involved, I thought they were deserving of inclusion.

While I was writing this book, the Great Flood of 2013 washed though Southern Alberta. It disrupted all of Calgary and the surrounding area for a number of weeks, and many people were impacted longer, some likely for life. The same can be said of the restaurant industry. Some were closed for a week or two, losing all their food and supplies. Others, like River Café, Manuel Latruwe and Vin Room in Mission, took longer to come back. At press time, Wurst was slated to be out for months while they rebuilt the kitchen, and both Il Gallo Nero and Lion's Den, sadly, had unknown fates due to devastating damage. Summer 2013 was not a good time for many.

• • •

Here are some of the specifics on the book you're holding. It's a collection of reviews on almost 300 eateries and food-related businesses that I like in Calgary and Southern Alberta. More than half of them are new since the last edition, a testimony to the vibrancy of the local food scene. (And there are lots more good ones reviewed in the 2nd edition of *My Favourite Cheap Eats*.)

This book has been divided into two main sections: "Big Eats" and "Little Eats." Big Eats contains full reviews of restaurants, while Little Eats offers shorter ones, mainly on places that specialize in specific aspects of the food industry such as cheese, baking, chocolate, ice cream and so on. There's also a short "Coffee (and Tea, too)" section starting on page 174, after the "Dining in Downtown Calgary" map.

Here are more details:

- Each section is arranged alphabetically, and all establishments appear at least twice in "The Lists" index at the back.
- Each establishment located downtown is marked with the Downtown Calgary logo. The map on page 172 also pinpoints all downtown locations.
- Credit card abbreviations are as follows: **V** stands for Visa; **MC**, MasterCard; **AE**, American Express; and **JCB**, Japan Credit Bureau.
- Noise levels are described with a loudspeaker symbol: ◁ means the room is nicely quiet; ◁) indicates talking is easy; ◁)) signifies you have to raise your voice to be heard; and ◁))) tells you the place is darn loud.
- Cost categories are based on a meal for two, with appetizers, main courses and desserts (or equivalent) and include GST but not drinks or gratuities: **$** means under $40; **$$** ranges from $40 to $70; **$$$** covers over $70 to $100; and **$$$$** pushes over $100.
- Facebook, Twitter and Instagram logos are included for establishments that have a presence on those social media.

"Eight gives you everything—wealth, long life, good fortune," a Chinese-Canadian friend said to me recently, explaining the numerical significance of eight in her culture. So with the hope that this eighth edition brings you a wealth of fine food options, a long life to sample them and the good fortune to enjoy each and every meal, let's get eating!

*John Gilchrist*
*Calgary, Alberta*
*August 2013*

# Aida's | Lebanese

**F**IVE in a row. That's how many times I've started a book with a review of Aida's.

And for good reasons. The most obvious is that Aida's starts with an *A* (though it's pronounced I-da), which increases the likelihood of it being first out the gate in a book organized alphabetically. But I also like to lead off with a consistently good restaurant, and this Mission landmark has maintained high quality in both the food and the experience since opening in 2000. And then there's Aida herself, a lovely lady who's always concerned that her customers have an excellent time.

Aida introduced me to mouhammara, the red pepper, walnut and pomegranate dip. It's so rich and robust, I can't eat here without having it. Or without having the best fattoush salad around: tart with lemon, savoury with sumac and crunchy with pita chips. (I still get a kick out of the way the word sounds—fattoush. Nice, eh?) I'm a kebab kind of guy, too. I'll take meat on a stick any day. At Aida's, the lamb and the chicken kebabs are my faves. Spiced with curry and oregano (the lamb) or garlic and lemon (the chicken), they're savoury and delightful. I like Aida's fatayer (pastries filled with spinach) and kibbeh (balls of cracked wheat and beef filled with beef and almonds), and her lentil soup and couscous entrees, too.

In fact, I don't remember ever leaving Aida's less than happy. That's why Aida's is still number one in my book. Literally.

**Address**
2208 – 4 Street SW

**Phone**
403.541.1189

**Hours**
Monday
11 am – 9 pm

Tuesday – Thursday
11 am – 10 pm

Friday & Saturday
11 am – 10:30 pm

**Reservations**
Highly recommended, especially weekends

**Cards**
V, MC, AE, Debit

**Drinks**
Full bar
No corkage

**Outdoor Dining**
None

**Noise**
🔊 – 🔊)

**Price Range**
$ – $$$

**Website**
aidasbistro.ca

# Alloy

**S**INCE opening in late 2007, Alloy has gone through all the phases of a hot new restaurant in an odd location.

As people wondered how an eatery would fare on the same strip as Timber Town and a big grocery warehouse, the first phase was, "You're opening a restaurant where?" Then as the culinary cognoscenti touted it as the new must-go-to joint, up next was, "Oh, my goodness! Have you been to Alloy?" Soon came the barrage of corporate events and weddings as word spread, not only about Alloy's unique "world-influenced" cuisine, but also about its engaging service and atmosphere. Later things moved on to maturity and a certain "Oh yes, we go to Alloy all the time" for some and an "Oh, I haven't been back to Alloy for ages, but I love that place" for others.

Ah, the phases of a restaurant's life, all in under six years.

Regardless, Alloy works. The location, just east of Macleod Trail on 42nd Avenue SE, is off the beaten track yet still accessible. And there's parking, the ne plus ultra for Calgary restaurants. The space itself helps. It's gorgeous. A California-industrial bungalow draped in white with lots of walnut, it's airy, light and perfect for wedding pictures, especially if the weather is good and the patio is lush.

And the food. The way Rogelio Herrera combines the flavours of global cultures— duck pâté and duck chorizo; lamb chops with carrot tahini and Balkan yogurt; calamari with aioli and Thai chili salsa—is inspired.

So we're now into the next phase of maturity, as in, "Oh, yeah, I can count on Alloy. It's a gem."

**Address**
220 – 42 Avenue SE

**Phone**
403.287.9255

**Hours**
Monday – Friday
11:30 am – 2 pm

Daily
5 pm – close

**Reservations**
Recommended

**Cards**
V, MC, AE, Debit

**Drinks**
Full bar
Corkage $30/bottle
or bring 1, buy 1

**Outdoor Dining**
Patio

**Noise**
🔊 – 🔊

**Price Range**
$$ – $$$$

**Website**
alloydining.com

# Anju | Modern Korean

**T**HIS is a weird review. Take a look at the sidebar to the right. A little sparse isn't it? Sorry about that, but let me explain. Anju closed their original restaurant in late June 2013, and by the time this book went to press, they had yet to find a new location. Seems that when their lease ran out, they decided to move to a higher-traffic area. Check their website, and by now, there might be a new location listed.

I included Anju here because I didn't want you to miss some of the most innovative, tasty and sometimes outrageous food available in Calgary. Roy Oh, the chef and mastermind behind Anju, combines his Korean heritage and his Canadian culinary upbringing in ways I've never seen from anyone else: kimchi jambalaya with lap cheong sausages, nori and a poached egg; panko-crusted tofu with sautéed kimchi and citrus aioli; spicy salmon tacos with sesame slaw; truffled yam fries with gochugaru (ground red chili) aioli; gochugaru- and caramel-crusted sablefish. The list could go on and on. Oh is always creating some new, intensely flavoured dish. This is the kind of food I always hope the next generation of contemporary-focused chefs will create from whatever heritage they've descended.

Anju's food jumps in your mouth, but it's also pretty on the plate. Oh, a former graphic designer, knows how to construct a plate to look good.

Oh promises the new Anju will continue this legacy. When it does (likely by early 2014), please fill in those TBA spots in the sidebar. It'll be a place you're going to want to go again and again.

**Address**
TBA

**Phone**
TBA

**Hours**
TBA

**Reservations**
TBA

**Cards**
V, MC, AE, Debit

**Drinks**
Full bar
Corkage: available, cost TBA

**Outdoor Dining**
TBA

**Noise**
TBA

**Price Range**
$ – $$$

**Website**
anju.ca

# Aroma | Mexican

**A**FTER a hard day of hiking or skiing in the Canmore area, it's time to refuel with some good grub. So how about Mexican? Perhaps not the first idea to come to mind in the Rockies, but a good one nonetheless, especially if you're thinking of Aroma.

Now located at the west end of Canmore's Main Street, Aroma started out as a sublet in Zona's restaurant space. Zona's did dinner, while Aroma did breakfast and lunch. Aroma proved so popular, it finally opened its own space full time.

Aroma serves some of the best Mexican food in this book. From guacamole with house-made tortilla chips and ceviche of basa in fresh lime to rellenos poblanos stuffed with goat cheese and cochinita pibil of pork tenderloin in a smoky achiote sauce, it's the real deal. Owners Jose Castillo and Laura Matamoros are proud of their Mexican heritage and they handcraft every meal. (The menu does wander into Tex-Mex fare with a list of fajitas, but hey, that's close.)

I'm fond of the enchiladas Norteñas where fresh-made corn tortillas are wrapped around slow-cooked, tender lamb, baked with an ancho chili sauce and sprinkled with goat cheese ($23). The flavours are rich and rustic, smoky and lively. Perfect for rehydrating with a margarita.

The owners have done a good job on Mexicanizing the space, too. In contrast with all the mountain-chic Canmore restaurants, colourful tablecloths and weavings, Mexican ceramics and mariachi music enliven the room here.

It's great to have some multicultural variety in the Bow Valley. And it's even better that the quality is so high.

**Address**
837 Main Street
Canmore

**Phone**
403.675.9913

**Hours**
Monday – Thursday
11 am – 3 pm
5 pm – 10 pm

Friday – Sunday
8 am – 10 pm

**Reservations**
Accepted in winter

**Cards**
V, MC, AE, Debit

**Drinks**
Full bar
No corkage

**Outdoor Dining**
Small patio

**Noise**
🔊

**Price Range**
$$ – $$$

**Website**
aromamexicanrestaurant.com

# Atlas

**A**LMOST every culture has some sort of meat on a stick: there's Malaysian satay, Brazilian churrascaria, Italian rosticini, even the humble Stampede corndog. But few do meat on a stick better than the Persians with their wonderful kebabs. At Atlas, there are the flame-broiled koobideh (ground beef), joojeh (chicken) and barg (beef strip loin), all served over saffron-tinged basmati with roasted tomatoes and onions. And they're terrific—juicy, flavourful, lean tasting. They do salmon ones and veggie versions, too.

If kebabs were all Atlas did, that would likely be enough. But kebabs are just one corner of the menu. There are great appetizer dips flavoured with fried eggplant or yogurt with wild shallots or spinach with fried onions. And then there are the khoresht dishes, slow-cooked stews that combine the unique flavours of Persia. You'll find ghormeh sabzi of kidney beans and beef sirloin, fesenjoon of walnuts, pomegranate paste and chicken, and karafs of celery, tofu and sour plums in an herb broth. (Note: Many of the ingredients are available in Atlas' attached market.)

Atlas' desert-toned setting works with the food. And with the groups that frequent the place. Tables are constantly being pulled together as groups dive into big piles of rice, bowls of khoresht and huge platters of kebabs. Atlas is very social, too, with chat fuelled by tea that's served as soon as you arrive.

Another note: Atlas does not serve any form of alcohol. So enjoy the tea. Or the pomegranate juice. Or, if you're into the full cultural experience, the yogurt drink called doogh.

But for sure, have some meat on a stick.

**Address**
1000 – 9 Avenue SW

**Phone**
403.230.0990

**Hours**
Tuesday – Thursday, Sunday
11 am – 8 pm

Friday & Saturday
11 am – 9 pm

**Reservations**
Recommended,
especially weekends

**Cards**
V, MC, AE, Debit

**Drinks**
No alcoholic beverages

**Outdoor Dining**
None

**Noise**
◁

**Price Range**
$$

**Website**
atlascalgary.com

downtown
calgary

# Avec Bistro

Contemporary French Bistro

**W**HILE the word "bistro" is attached to many a local eatery, few honour the true French meaning of the word like Avec Bistro does. A bistro should be light and lively, animated by conversation over a sip of wine or rich coffee and energized with great food. That's Avec, the place to go for classic bistro fare: steak frites, beef tartare, mussels, bouillabaisse, duck confit, and on and on. Cooked slowly with care and fine ingredients, the food at Avec Bistro is, frankly, better than a lot of what we've had in France lately.

Avec consumes the corner of 5th Street and 11th Avenue SW with grace and charm. The room is split into two sections seating sixty-six, with an additional six seats at a zinc bar. In an age of noisy eateries, Avec is refreshingly calm. Not somnolent—they tend to play French rock 'n' roll—but it's mature and relaxed and not nearly as frenetic as many.

Avec's maturity also comes through in the service, even though it only opened in 2012. Avec is a partnership of five restaurant professionals; at any given time, there'll be a least a couple of them there. That seasoned skill is a comfort—there's no worry, for example, that someone else will get your dish.

Because you wouldn't want your seared foie gras with toasted brioche and house-made preserves to go astray. Or your steak frites draped in Béarnaise to go walkabout. If it landed on someone else's table, it might be consumed before anyone notices.

And who could blame the lucky recipient? Good bistro food is hard to refuse. And Avec's is among the best.

**Address**
105, 550 – 11 Avenue SW

**Phone**
587.352.0964

**Hours**
Monday – Friday
11:30 am – 2:30 pm

Monday – Thursday
5 pm – 10 pm

Friday & Saturday
5 pm – 11 pm

Sunday
5 pm – 9 pm

**Reservations**
Accepted

**Cards**
V, MC, AE, Debit

**Drinks**
Full bar
Call for corkage details

**Outdoor Dining**
Patio

**Noise**
◁) – ◁))

**Price Range**
$$ – $$$$

**Website**
avecbistro.com

# The Banffshire Club

Upscale Canadian

**D**INING at the Fairmont Banff Springs offers a baffling list of choices. There's Italian, Japanese, German, traditional Canadian and even a golf course restaurant. Each has its own unique atmosphere and attitude; I'm especially fond of the multi-purpose Bow Valley Grill. But the restaurant the Springs calls their signature dining room—the Banffshire Club—is one of the smallest and most hidden in the 125-year-old Castle on the Bow.

Created when the Springs underwent a major renovation and expansion around the turn of the century, it replicates the Stuart era of Scotland with its curved ceilings, heavy leathered chairs and tartan decor. A (usually) quiet hideaway in the busy hotel, it seats about 60 in cloistered comfort.

The menu features high-end Canadian seasonal cuisine that includes farro cooked into a risotto-like dish along with foraged mushrooms, black kale and Sylvan Star Gouda ($26), and spot prawns and squid prepared with Mennonite sausage, a quail egg, cabbage and apples ($14 appetizer). There's a 22-ounce slab of Angus prime rib carved tableside and served with asparagus, more of those mushrooms and whipped, organic Ambra potatoes ($95 for two). It's interesting stuff.

It all comes with an outstanding wine list, a 33-page encyclopedia that ranges from fine Canadian wines to Bordeaux that reach back to the 1970s. And while many of the rare wines splurge into the thousands of dollars, there are some tasty bargains on the list, too.

The Banffshire can be a great dining choice. Not necessarily an everyday place with its prices and stately setting, but fabulous when you feel like being pampered.

**Address**
405 Spray Avenue
(The Fairmont Banff Springs)
Banff

**Phone**
403.762.6860

**Hours**
Tuesday – Saturday
6 pm – 9 pm

**Reservations**
Recommended

**Cards**
V, MC, AE, JCB, Debit

**Drinks**
Full bar
No corkage

**Outdoor Dining**
None

**Noise**
◁ – ◁)

**Price Range**
$$$$

**Website**
fairmont.com/banff-springs

# Bar C

**C**ANADIAN Rocky Mountain Resorts (CRMR) has brought us many fine restaurants over the years: Cilantro, Divino, the Ranche, Sleeping Buffalo in Banff, and on and on. They'd been quiet for a while, but in the winter of 2013, they opened Bar C next to Cilantro. And it's very different from anything they've done before.

First off, Bar C is a bar. Second, it has an industrial look instead of the usual CRMR elegant rusticity of elk-horn chandeliers and such. It is a large, square, open room with two actual bars: one for beverages, the other for oysters and charcuterie. The chairs are metal, the floors, concrete and the room dividers, metal girders. It's highlighted by LED lighting strips and filled with televisions and an omnipresent sound system. So Bar C is, in fact, a bar, but very much a bar of today.

It also houses a serious kitchen with serious cooks. They make an outstanding Hawaiian poke of tuna marinated in a soy-lime dressing and then topped with toasted sesame seeds, crisp wontons and a seaweed salad. When was the last time you ordered raw tuna in a bar? Or a beet salad? They make theirs with goat cheese, candied walnuts and a balsamic glaze. This is bar food?

Some of the food keys on CRMR's own elk, bison and deer, which appears, for example, in the charcuterie, the meatballs, the tartare (bison) and the carpaccio (elk). The food is richly flavoured, attractively plated and skilfully served. If this is bar food, I say let's see more of it in town.

**Address**
340 – 17 Avenue SW

**Phone**
403.984.3667

**Hours**
Monday – Friday
4 pm – close

Saturday
11 am – close

**Reservations**
Accepted for groups
of 8 – 16 only

**Cards**
V, MC, AE, Discovery,
Debit

**Drinks**
Full bar
No corkage

**Outdoor Dining**
2 patios

**Noise**
◁)) – ◁)))

**Price Range**
$$ – $$$

**Website**
bar-c.ca

# The Bavarian Inn

Bavarian & Rocky Mountain Cuisine

**F**OLLOWING the Great Flood of 2013, the first restaurant to reopen in the devastated Bragg Creek area was the Bavarian Inn. An old riverbed that runs behind the restaurant diverted the water away from the restaurant, leaving them with only a metre of seepage water to pump out of their basement. They were up and running within a week.

The Bavarian Inn, opened in 1976, is nestled in a forest of tall spruce trees. It's seen a few different owners, the current being German ex-pat Joseph Wiewer, the former executive chef at Bonterra and the now-closed Wildwood. Wiewer took it over in the summer of 2011 and has maintained the Black Forest meets Rocky Mountain tone. So you'll find the requisite schnitzels and sausages, but you'll also find elk in a sour cherry and ginger sauce, and bison flank steak marinated in rosemary, black pepper and olive oil, served with a chimichurri sauce.

Plus you'll find fine spaetzle, some of the best red cabbage and sauerkraut I've had, and skilful preparation throughout. The jäger schnitzel, for example, which features thin pieces of veal, is cooked to order and is simply sliced here (it's often pre-cooked and pounded elsewhere). There are seafood and vegetarian options, too, allowing alternatives to the typically hearty (and sometimes heavy) fare.

You'll find excellent service here. Staff are casual but professional, straddling the needs of tourists and locals alike, those who come for big family events and those who are just refueling while passing through. Either way, it's a fine—and dry—dining destination.

**Address**
75 White Avenue
Bragg Creek

**Phone**
403.949.3611

**Hours**
Tuesday – Friday
11:30 am – 3 pm
4:45 pm – 8 pm

Saturday & Sunday
11:30 am – 9 pm

**Reservations**
Recommended weekends

**Cards**
V, MC, AE, Debit

**Drinks**
Full bar
Corkage $15/bottle

**Outdoor Dining**
Deck

**Noise**
🔊

**Price Range**
$$$

**Website**
thebavarianinn.com

# Belgo

Belgian-Inspired Brasserie

**I**F you want to take the temperature of Calgary's oil and gas sector, you need go no farther than the bar at Belgo. How long do the young O&G workers linger over lunch? How pricey are the beverages they're buying? What kind of budget are they throwing at after-work events? If the corporate credit cards are flying, we're OK. If not, watch out. Chances are, it'll be pretty busy regardless—things just get kicked to a higher level of intensity when oil and gas prices are up.

Belgo is a huge place—almost 400 seats—and keys on a Belgian-focused list of 50 craft beers that includes a number of other European and Canadian beers, too. But Belgo is about more than beer. Managing partner and executive chef Shaun Desaulniers is a talent, one of the few who can manage a hopping bar and a good restaurant at the same time. He oversees a menu of international taste treats, inspired by Belgian brasserie cuisine, that rambles from bulgogi cheesesteak sandwiches and Thai curried lobster with mussels, clams, scallops and shrimp (a lively take on bouillabaisse) to bacon-wrapped chicken ballotine and piri-piri tiger shrimp.

It's a smart menu that keeps many items under $20, with a six-ounce beef tenderloin served with gratin dauphinois, truffled mushroom duxelles and port jus topping things out at $36. Belgo even has an appetizer list of lamb meatballs, tempura vegetables, tuna poke and shrimp-bacon flatbread for $5 each. Two or three of these make a nice meal. With a Belgian brew, of course.

**Address**
501 – 8 Avenue SW

**Phone**
403.265.6555

**Hours**
Monday & Tuesday
7 am – midnight

Wednesday – Friday
7 am – 2 am

Saturday
5 pm – 2 am

**Reservations**
Recommended

**Cards**
V, MC, AE, Debit

**Drinks**
Full bar
Corkage $25/bottle

**Outdoor Dining**
Patio

**Noise**
🔊) – 🔊))

**Price Range**
$ – $$$$

**Website**
belgo.ca

downtown calgary

# The Belvedere

Contemporary
North American

I F you're looking for a place to hold a small corporate dinner or celebrate a special occasion, the Belvedere may well fit the bill. The historic sandstone building with the huge skylight looking up at the Calgary Tower, the cozy lounge and the pristine dining room gives a sense of solidity and richness to any meal. The Belvedere looks like it's been there forever, yet is as fresh and modern as they come.

The Belvedere's menu matches this timeless yet current tone with its duo of lamb rack and braised lamb shoulder served with a lemon verbena three-bean salad and crispy mint ($42), its elk chop with black truffle jus and a vegetable bubble and squeak ($44), and its poached Atlantic lobster tail with a lemon and fennel salad ($32). This is intriguing food: there are frog legs ($14) and even free-range rabbits with artichoke purée and tempura polenta ($39). If you're looking for foie gras, it is always here.

But the food at the Belvedere is not esoteric. Precisely prepared and expertly served, it is always satisfying. Here, the customer comes first. A lunchtime croque monsieur of toasted brioche, house-smoked Broek Pork ham and cave-aged Gruyère ($18) is delightful. They even have a three-course, $25 lunch menu that will have you in and out in under and hour.

Not that you want to rush a meal at the Belvedere. It's worth kicking back with a wine from their cellar of over 750 selections and enjoying the surroundings. It'll give you a whole new perspective on the Calgary Tower.

**Address**
107 Stephen Avenue SW

**Phone**
403.265.9595

**Hours**
Monday – Friday
11:30 am – 2 pm

Monday – Saturday
4:30 pm – 10 pm

**Reservations**
Recommended

**Cards**
V, MC, AE, Debit

**Drinks**
Full bar
Corkage $25/bottle,
1st bottle free

**Outdoor Dining**
Patio

**Noise**
◁ – ◁))

**Price Range**
$$ – $$$$

**Website**
thebelvedere.ca

downtown
calgary

# Big Fish

**I** ASK about the lamb and lobster burger served on a herbed ciabatta bun with Cambozola, avocado and salsa. The server's eyes widen as she says, "It's a monster with big chunks of lobster on top of the lamb patty. With the bun, it's a challenge to eat."

Sounds like a fish story to me, appropriate for the nautical setting at Big Fish, the seafaring sister of Open Range. While the light shines down on my menu from encased boat lamps overhead, I look deeper into the briny depths of the menu.

"How about the chowdah?" I ask, a New England dialect suddenly creeping into my speech. "Or the mussels in the white wine, leek and green curry sauce?"

"Both excellent," she replies. "Those are the two dishes I recommend the most."

I opt for the mussels and a capricious, last-minute choice: the Niçoise salad with baby potatoes, yellow beets, sun-dried olives and crispy white anchovies, plus three barely seared slices of albacore tuna. Catherine has a pair of dense crab and shrimp cakes, declaring them to be good, not crumbly as in many other places, though in need of more citrus caper aioli. The Niçoise is good, too—fresh, brightly dressed, perfectly seared fish.

But it's the mussels that impress the most. The broth is creamy and delicious, perfect for dipping the toasted Sidewalk Citizen bread in. Very little makes its way back to the kitchen. And the mussels! Huge, I tells ya. Mammoth West Coast mussels, bursting from their over-sized shells, tender as soft butter, tasty as they get. Big, beautiful mollusks.

And that's no fish story.

**Address**
1112 Edmonton Trail NE

**Phone**
403.277.3403

**Hours**
Monday – Friday
11:30 am – 10 pm

Saturday
10 am – 10 pm

Sunday
9 am – 10 pm

**Reservations**
Highly recommended

**Cards**
V, MC, AE, Debit

**Drinks**
Full bar
Corkage $20/bottle
Free corkage Wednesdays

**Outdoor Dining**
Patio

**Noise**
🔉 – 🔊

**Price Range**
$$ – $$$

**Website**
big-fish.ca

# Big Rock Grill

**I**N 1997, when Big Rock opened its new brewery and restaurant in the western reaches of the city, it stood all alone in a field. You could see it for miles. And with the restaurant being the only one in the area, it was very popular. Then warehouses, fast-food outlets and industrial structures grew up around the brewery, hiding the green-topped buildings from passersby. But because of the beer-themed decor, the food of chef Klaus Wöckinger and a long bar that poured the freshest Big Rock possible, the grill remained popular.

But time marches on and at the time of writing this book, Big Rock Grill was undergoing major changes. Wöckinger had retired, decamping to Kelowna. New owners Harry Griesser and Markus Aschauer had taken over the restaurant, and together with Big Rock, were in the process of renovating the 100-seat room. The plan, which should be complete by the time you read this, was to create a comfy, contemporary pub-like atmosphere with banquettes and booths, padded leather seats and that long bar, renoed to have a rustic, beer-keg tone but still featuring Big Rock's products.

I slipped in for a pleasant lunch before the wrecking ball hit and found that Griesser (formerly of Canmore's tasty Railway Deli) and Aschauer (who owned a Canmore catering company) have kept the Continentally inspired, contemporary fare. So my minestrone was still hearty, a chicken pot pie was laced with vegetables and chunks of chicken, and the cheesecake was thick and saucy with strawberries, a creamy-rich finish to my meal. You, of course, may want to finish with a brew instead. Nothing wrong with that.

**Address**
5555 – 76 Avenue SE
(Big Rock Brewery)

**Phone**
403.236.1606

**Hours**
Monday – Friday
11 am – 2:30 pm

(Available for private evening functions)

**Reservations**
Recommended

**Cards**
V, MC, AE, Debit

**Drinks**
Full bar
No corkage

**Outdoor Dining**
Patio

**Noise**
◁ – ◁)

**Price Range**
$ – $$

**Website**
bigrockgrill.com

# Bistro Provence

French

**B**UILT in 1882, the old Sheep River Post Office served the community of Okotoks for over 60 years. Then the tin-clad building sat empty for a while before resurfacing as a French restaurant a few decades ago. It's changed hands several times since, but has always remained French. Which fits the tone. Bistro Provence feels like the little French bistros we love to find while cruising the back roads of France.

Bistro Provence has two distinct characters: one for night, one for day. And it has two dining rooms to accommodate each. The old section is set for dinner, while the newer annex is used for the lunch crowd (it doubles as dinner overflow, too).

The lunch menu features quiche, sandwiches and a burger, plus salads such as the one with beets, salmon, fennel, mango and mandarin oranges, with all dishes well under $20. A croque madame—two slices of house-baked bread layered with sliced ham and cheese, all smothered in béchamel sauce and topped with a fried egg—was as close to a perfect sandwich as I've had. Even the green salad served with it was great, dressed thoroughly as it was with a lively dressing. And a simple carrot-ginger soup nearly redefined my understanding of this dish. Creamy, carroty, light on the ginger and topped with fresh, raw peas, slivered carrots and cheese, and crunchy croutons, each spoonful was a dance of flavours and textures. Lovely.

At night, the tone kicks up with the likes of saddle of rabbit ($42) and banana leaf-wrapped baked halibut ($34). Elegant food in a rustic setting. *Très bonnes.*

**Address**
52 North Railway Street
Okotoks

**Phone**
403.938.2224

**Hours**
Tuesday – Saturday
11 am – 2 pm
5:30 pm – close

**Reservations**
Recommended

**Cards**
V, MC, AE, Debit

**Drinks**
Full bar
Corkage $30/bottle

**Outdoor Dining**
Patio

**Noise**
◁) – ◁))

**Price Range**
$ – $$$$

**Website**
bistro-provence.ca

# Bistro Rouge

**Regional Bistro**

**Address**
1919 Sirocco Drive SW

**Phone**
403.514.0561

**Hours**
Saturday & Sunday
11 am – 2 pm

Daily
5 pm – close
(opens 4 pm for
cocktails & charcuterie)

**Reservations**
Recommended

**Cards**
V, MC, AE, Debit

**Drinks**
Full bar
No corkage

**Outdoor Dining**
None

**Noise**
◁))

**Price Range**
$$ – $$$

**Website**
bistrorougeyyc.com

Olivier Reynaud and Paul Rogalski, the proprietors of the estimable Rouge in Inglewood, have been looking for a second location for years. Not one that exactly replicated Rouge, but one where they could present a more casual, bistro style of food. In early 2013, they finally found a spot they liked on the west side of Sarcee Trail, just south of 17th Avenue SW.

The space, formerly a series of ho-hum eateries, was renovated into a contemporary, four-room bistro that revolves around a central, open kitchen. Two of the rooms face east over Sarcee toward downtown, the third flanks the kitchen and the fourth houses a lively lounge. The look is simple and clean, with black and white photos adorning the walls.

There's some uniqueness to the food: a velouté "bar" offers freshly made velouté soups in choices of spinach, blue cheese, mushroom, beet or garlic confit. Choose one or whatever combination you'd like and a large Mason jar will arrive piping hot at your table. (I like the mushroom-blue cheese combo.) Bistro Rouge also features grilled paillards, flattened pieces of beef sirloin or chicken breast or pork loin, seasoned and grilled.

And then there's the roast chicken with fine herbs, available both in-house and as an order-to-pick-up option. Given Bistro Rouge's location at the edge of western suburbia, takeout is a natural. You can get a whole chicken plus two sides that will feed four people for $44—not a bad deal, especially considering the stellar quality.

But then again, dining in includes excellent service. It's a tough call.

# Bistro 2210

Contemporary Bistro

**I**F we were walking along rue Saint-Dominique in Paris and came across a restaurant called Bistro 2210 (*vingt-deux dix, peut-être*), we'd think, "Hmmm—quaint place, typical French bistro, nice menu of classics, decent prices." We might also think, "Wow, these tables are quite widely spaced. Lots of room here."

Bistro 2210 is certainly not a big place at only 42 seats, but if it were really in France, there would be at least 60 seats shoehorned in. (There'd be a row of tables on the sidewalk outside, too.)

But we Canadians like our elbow room, so chef/owner Jason Armstrong and his crew have given us plenty. But they haven't compromised one cornichon on the food. From bouillabaisse and escargots vol-au-vent to beef bourguignon and moules frites, it's French all the way.

Well, almost. There are a few Canadian variations on the menu. The macaroni au gratin is made with Sylvan Star Gouda, the salade Lyonnaise has smoked salmon and the steak frites feature a fine Alberta beef flatiron cut. (Thanks heavens, because most French beef can't compare.) If you want a burger, few are better than 2210's lamb burger with rosemary goat cheese and a brioche bun.

The pricing at 2210 is very appealing. The steak frites are $21, as is the bouillabaisse, and the burger is $16—pretty reasonable when you look elsewhere.

With this quality and pricing, not to mention the pleasant service and roomy confines, Bistro 2210 is a calm, comfortable neighbourhood place. And it doesn't require a trip to France.

**Address**
2210 – 4 Street SW

**Phone**
403.228.4528

**Hours**
Saturday & Sunday
10 am – 2 pm

Tuesday – Friday
Noon – 10 pm

Saturday
5 pm – 10 pm

**Reservations**
Accepted

**Cards**
V, MC, AE, Debit

**Drinks**
Full bar
No corkage

**Outdoor Dining**
None

**Noise**
◁ – ◁)

**Price Range**
$$ – $$$

**Website**
bistro2210.com

# Blink

French-Influenced Regional

Y OU know that Calgary tradition of riding a horse into a hotel or restaurant any time there's a major event like the Stampede or the Grey Cup? That started at this address during the 1923 Stampede when cowboy Eddie King took his horse on a stroll through what was then the Club Café.

Home to Blink since 2007 and one of the widest of the historic downtown brick and sandstone buildings, the space has been restored and renovated into a lovely dining room. A long bar runs about halfway along one wall, a long banquette lines the other and a bright open kitchen fills the far end.

Blink features regional ingredients prepared with French technique. A salad of buffalo mozzarella, fresh fava beans and torn bread ($14.50) comes with a burnt walnut paste that ties it all together. (I know, burnt walnuts may not sound terribly appealing, but this French *bien cuit* approach really works here.) An early summer salad brings together asparagus, English peas, broad beans, thin-sliced beets, hazelnuts, a Scotch (quail) egg, and a goat milk purée ($14.50) in a wonderfully fresh combination. And a fillet of chinook salmon with Parmesan polenta, tomato fondue, spinach and a Niçoise ratatouille ($29.50) is a delightful dish, complex and earthy at the same time.

Proprietor Leslie Echino will pair your food beautifully with her thoughtful wine list if you'd like. And don't dare miss dessert—it's among the best in town.

So Blink's food is smartly conceived and expertly executed. These are delicate plates (in flavour, not quantity) that will definitely command your attention.

Just save a little something in case a horse drops in.

**Address**
111 Stephen Avenue SW

**Phone**
403.263.5330

**Hours**
Monday – Thursday
11 am – 10 pm

Friday
11 am – 11 pm

Saturday
5 pm – 11 pm

**Reservations**
Accepted

**Cards**
V, MC, AE, Debit

**Drinks**
Full bar
Corkage $20/bottle

**Outdoor Dining**
Small patio

**Noise**
◁ – ◁))

**Price Range**
$$$ – $$$$

**Website**
blinkcalgary.com

downtown calgary

# Blondes | Diner & Bistro

**T**HE already crowded Mission dining scene got more crowded in the spring of 2013 with the opening of Blondes Diner. New owners took over the rotating-door space that has seen everything over the past 20 years, from pie shops and Greek restaurants to Mexican joints and dicey bars, and they've made some good upgrades. So Blondes looks like it might stick around for a while.

The biggest indicator is that they actually installed some serious kitchen equipment in the restaurant, something no one else had really done. They also gave the place a full facelift, redoing it in a white and black theme. About the only thing they kept is the well-worn terra cotta tile floor. Now around 80 seats cover that floor, and a bar—also semi-original—fills one corner. On warm days, a patio brightens the sidewalk side of Blondes.

Blondes has adopted a breakfast and lunch diner theme that keys on high-quality, local ingredients. The croque madame is built on Sidewalk Citizen sourdough and topped with pulled Broek Pork ham. The kale and tomato salad served with the sandwich is made from local hothouse- and field-grown vegetables. Each dish is made to-order, so there's nice attention to detail. They even do a house-made ketchup.

As this book was going to press, Blondes had plans to expand into the evening hours with more diner classics. That should give the kitchen more breadth. And help conquer the curse of the location.

**Address**
2005B – 4 Street SW

**Phone**
403.474.3867

**Hours**
Daily
8 am – 4 pm

**Reservations**
Accepted until 10:30 am

**Cards**
V, MC, AE, Debit

**Drinks**
Full bar
Corkage TBA

**Outdoor Dining**
Patio

**Noise**
◁) – ◁))

**Price Range**
$$

**Website**
blondesdiner.com

# Boccavino | Italian Lounge & Grill

Lina's Italian Market is one of the most popular places around town for Italian (and Mediterranean) ingredients and accessories. It makes a nice spot for a quick lunch, too. (Just the act of buying Parmigiano and prosciutto makes me hungry.)

But if you'd like a lengthier repast, step next door to Boccavino, Lina's Italian lounge and grill. Drawing from Lina's warehouse of ingredients, Boccavino is able to provide fresh Italian foods prepared in traditional Southern Italian style. Pizzas, pastas, bruschetta and veal dishes roll out of the sparkling kitchen just like in a Calabrian village.

The pizzas are medium crusted, bathed in a light layer of San Marzano tomato sauce, topped with excellent cold cuts and cheeses, and usually served blisteringly hot. It's great pizza. The pastas are plated in huge mounds, liberally sauced and sent out steaming. There's no pretense to light dining here. You want pasta? You'll get pasta. And lots of it. The veal is thin cut, quick fried and abundantly sauced, adding to the feast-like atmosphere. And for the non-Italian fan, there are nachos, dry ribs, chicken wings and a Boccavino burger. This is still a lounge, after all.

And fitting with that lounge concept is a casual tone to the service. Which also fits with the surroundings. Boccavino is dimly lit and focused around a large, central bar, giving it a tone that looks back to the 1960s, albeit with a bank of flat-screen televisions. And with prices that are reminiscent of pre-millennium years, it's all the more attractive.

**Address**
2220 Centre Street N

**Phone**
403.276.2030

**Hours**
Monday – Wednesday
11 am – 10 pm

Thursday – Saturday
11 am – 11 pm

Sunday
3:30 pm – 10 pm

**Reservations**
Accepted

**Cards**
V, MC, AE, Debit

**Drinks**
Full bar
Corkage $15/bottle

**Outdoor Dining**
4 tables

**Noise**
◁) – ◁))

**Price Range**
$$

**Website**
boccavino.com

# Bonterra

WHEN people ask about restaurants with good patios, one that's always near the top of my list is Bonterra. Tucked away from traffic, surrounded by high walls and jungled with flora of all sorts (in summer, anyway), Bonterra's patio is a prime ticket on a sunny day.

Bonterra is near the top of my list when it comes to finding good Italian food, too. Chef Glen Manzer has an outstanding handle on Italian cuisine, reinventing classics and infusing creativity into his menu.

Bonterra's linguine alla carbonara, for instance, has wild boar bacon and chilies to impart a rich earthiness to the dish. The panzanella salad includes freshly made fior di latte cheese along with grilled radicchio, crisp focaccia, fennel and an apple-anchovy vinaigrette, all elevating the traditional stale-bread appetizer. And who thought to combine calamari with golden raisins? Inspired.

I like the simplicity and intelligence of Bonterra's wine list, too. Spanning New World and Old World choices but leaning to the Italian palate, the concise list offers many wines by the glass or carafe.

Bonterra's interior is just as engaging as the patio, especially if you can snag a fireside seat on a frosty night. The high brick walls, the industrial concrete floors, the private room up a short set of stairs all bring a level of comfort to the dining experience. The decor, combined with all-round fine service and excellent food, helps remind me that Bonterra is more than a pretty patio. It's one of our great local restaurants.

And at press time, the Bonterra folks were in the process of opening Posto, a new bar and pizza joint next door.

**Address**
1016 – 8 Street SW

**Phone**
403.262.8480

**Hours**
Monday – Friday
11:30 am – 2 pm

Daily
5 pm – close

**Reservations**
Recommended

**Cards**
V, MC, AE, Debit

**Drinks**
Full bar
No corkage

**Outdoor Dining**
Patio

**Noise**
◁) – ◁))

**Price Range**
$$ – $$$

**Website**
bonterra.ca

# Borgo

Family-Style
Rustic Italian

**N**o restaurant is indicative of the change in the dining scene more than Borgo. Run by Giuseppe Di Gennaro, Borgo is a lively (read: loud) Italian restaurant where the food is great and nothing, aside from some large platters, costs more than $18. This is the same Di Gennaro who opened the outstanding (and now closed) Capo in 2006, the place where high-end Italian cuisine was served and where many appetizers surpassed $18. (And the mains? Big bucks.)

But Capo thrived in the last of the pre-recession days of "fine dining." Such restaurants were quiet and calm and serious. Nowadays those three words are out, having been replaced by lively and energetic and fun. That's Borgo. From the café tables that spill onto the patio and the marble-topped bar that fills the centre of the restaurant to the big booths that line the room and the long communal butcher-block tables that front the open kitchen, Borgo is packed with people and filled with energy.

The rich aromas of Di Gennaro's cooking roll out of the kitchen, and bowl after platter of orecchiette with smoked bacon and roasted garlic, veal meatballs with Grana Padano polenta, and charbroiled sirloins with truffle fries are hauled out to hungry diners. Borgo's is rich, hearty food, mostly served family style for sharing. (That is so not what Capo did.) Borgo even makes us waspy types feel like part of a big Italian family who have a very good cook in the kitchen. It's what dining is about these days.

We miss Capo, but welcome Borgo. It's a fair trade.

**Address**
818 – 16 Avenue SW

**Phone**
403.245.2202

**Hours**
Tuesday – Friday
10 am – close

Saturday & Sunday
10 am – 3 pm
5 pm – close

**Reservations**
Recommended weekends

**Cards**
V, MC, AE, Debit

**Drinks**
Full bar
Corkage: bring 1, buy 1

**Outdoor Dining**
Small patio

**Noise**
◁)) – ◁))

**Price Range**
$$ – $$$

**Website**
borgo.ca

# Boxwood

**W**HEN the City of Calgary redeveloped Central Memorial Park (great job!), they did a very smart thing. They constructed two buildings there, one to accommodate park business, the other to become a restaurant. Then they did another smart thing. They leased the second building to Sal Howell and the River Café team. The result is a River Café-light sort of place called Boxwood.

Boxwood is a tight, rectangular space that has been creatively designed to house a tiny, open kitchen with high bar seats arranged around the kitchen and more seats parked along the windows and at a high, central table. It's, shall we say, cozy. The seating isn't for everyone, but hit a warm, sunny day and there are few better seats in town than the ones on Boxwood's patio, around the corner from their own small produce garden.

The seasonal menu revolves—literally—around a large rotisserie at the back of the kitchen. At any time, there may be lamb legs or chickens or rolled porchettas spinning away on it, ready to be served up with roasted apples (porchetta) or radishes and kale (chicken) or fingerling potatoes and green beans (lamb leg). At reasonable prices, too, by River Café standards: $19 for each of the above.

The veg and fibre crowd are happy here, too, with lemon lentil dal, roasted parsnip and cauliflower soup, toasted quinoa with sunchokes and spinach, red lentil hummus and more. Some of these may seem a bit earnest, but they're very tasty, lovely choices. And so in keeping with the park setting outside. Very smart indeed.

**Address**
340 – 13 Avenue SW
(Central Memorial Park)

**Phone**
403.265.4006

**Hours**
Daily
11 am – 10 pm

**Reservations**
Not accepted

**Cards**
V, MC, Debit

**Drinks**
Full bar
Corkage $15/bottle
Free corkage Sundays

**Outdoor Dining**
Patio

**Noise**
◁ – ◁)

**Price Range**
$ – $$$

**Website**
boxwoodcafe.ca

# Brasserie Kensington

**Canadian Brasserie**

Cam Dobranski loves French food. Or perhaps more specifically, the chef/owner of Brasserie Kensington loves duck fat and foie gras. He's gone so far as to partner with Quebec's Brome Lake Ducks and Élisé Duck to feature their products on his menu.

He does the duck thing seriously, with deep fryers filled with duck fat, ready for his frites to take a dip. And he doesn't stop there. The French onion soup is done with duck stock, there's duck confit, duck rillette, duck gravy and duck breast. Even the bar-snack potato chips are fried in duck fat. On the foie gras side, it's sliced off torchons, popped on top of poutine and layered into Dobranski's take on nachos (the "foie-chos"). Foie even finds its way into a parfait served with red wine jelly and an ice cream blended with caramel and sea salt.

But Brasserie Kensington is not just about duck and duck liver. The compressed brasserie, perched above Dobranski's other restaurant, Wine Bar Kensington, also works up some tasty salads, steaks and seafoods. The hanger steak comes with a choice of four sauces (none of them duck based), and the bouillabaisse is seafood from broth to shell. With a list of poutines, sandwiches, mussels and oysters rounding out the list, this is a menu with huge appeal. Dobranski does a particularly good job on his soups (like the onion and the bouillabaisse) and his sauces (whatever they're poured on).

Maybe it's the duck fat that makes Brasserie Kensington so good. More likely, it's simply Dobranski's skill.

**Address**
1131 Kensington Road NW
(Second Floor)

**Phone**
403.457.4148

**Hours**
Tuesday – Friday
11:30 am – 10:30 pm

Saturday & Sunday
10 am – 11 pm

**Reservations**
Recommended

**Cards**
MC
ATM

**Drinks**
Full bar
No corkage

**Outdoor Dining**
None

**Noise**
🔊

**Price Range**
$$ – $$$

**Website**
brasseriekensington.com

# Brava Bistro

**Contemporary Bistro**

CONSISTENCY. It's the hardest thing to achieve in the restaurant biz. How often have you been to a place that was great one time and blah the next? It's difficult to be top-notch day after day.

But Brava Bistro manages the challenge well. Since 1999, it's been one of the most consistent, high-quality restaurants in the city. The lobster gnocchi, the crispy roasted chicken, the braised short ribs: time and again, superlative.

Not that I get to try them all that much. That's because we're frequenters of Brava's Sunday Supper, held on the first Sunday of each month. For a fixed price (usually $32, plus tax and tip), there's a choice from three appetizers, three mains and a couple of desserts. Sometimes regular menu items like the ones above appear as choices. But more often, the chefs roll out seasonal dishes or market-fresh ideas, simply letting their creativity wander. It's always worth the ticket price.

Much of Brava's consistency is linked to two key players, executive chef Kevin Turner and managing partner Dewey (yes, just Dewey), both of whom have been with Brava since the early days. Turner spent some time in the San Francisco area, learning the culinary ropes before landing here. His sensibility with California and Mediterranean cuisines is layered onto the menu: a grape and blue-cheese flatbread, an arugula salad with lemon vinaigrette, that pan-roasted crispy chicken. Dewey also oversees Brava's notable wine list. There are always great finds on it, including some that are a steal, and many available by the glass.

It all helps build the consistency that is often elusive elsewhere.

**Address**
723 – 17 Avenue SW

**Phone**
403.228.1854

**Hours**
Monday – Saturday
11:30 am – 3 pm

Sunday – Wednesday
5 pm – 10 pm

Thursday – Saturday
5 pm – midnight

**Reservations**
Recommended

**Cards**
V, MC, AE, Debit

**Drinks**
Full bar
Corkage $25/bottle

**Outdoor Dining**
Patio

**Noise**
◁) – ◁))

**Price Range**
$$ – $$$$

**Website**
bravabistro.com

# Briggs

Rustic Comfort Food

I HAVE always liked the warehousy locations along 10th Avenue. They make great restaurant spaces. And I really like what the team at Briggs has done with what once was Cannery Row.

The high-ceilinged, wood and brick room has been taken back to its essentials and revitalized with industrial-style hanging lamps, huge wooden tables and a gleaming open kitchen in one corner. A lounge fills one part of the big space while the dining area faces the kitchen.

The stars here are a pair of Josper ovens, fuelled by mesquite charcoal. These ovens can easily reach 700°F, and they have reduced venting so that smoke stays inside the chamber and permeates whatever is cooked in them. The room itself is not smoky, but the food is.

Especially the meats: beef short ribs, pork belly, prime rib, halibut, chicken, a big burger, the 48-ounce tomahawk rib-eye (so named because of the huge bone that extends from the rib-eye). Some items, though, such as the lobster ravioli, devilled eggs, poutine and calamari with fennel, arugula and tomato aioli, never see the ovens. That calamari dish is one of the best I've had— lightly battered and served with a creamy aioli for dipping.

And the prime rib sandwich is as tender as I could ever imagine. On a house-baked roll with horseradish butter and a bowl of jus, it redefines the beef dip. (At $17.25, it should.) It comes with crispy fries, soup or salad and will surely become a lunch of choice for many customers.

Watch for the desserts, too (lemon pie, chocolate cake, vanilla millefeuille)—they're fitting ends to the food and setting.

**Address**
317– 10 Avenue SW

**Phone**
587.350.5015

**Hours**
Sunday – Thursday
11 am – midnight

Friday & Saturday
11 am – 1 am

**Reservations**
Accepted for groups
of 6 or more

**Cards**
V, MC, AE, Debit

**Drinks**
Full bar
Corkage $20/bottle

**Outdoor Dining**
Patio

**Noise**

**Price Range**
$$$ – $$$$

**Website**
briggskandb.com

downtown calgary

# Broxburn Café

## Farm Fresh

**T**HERE is no restaurant in this book further from our Calgary house than Broxburn Café, located a few kilometres east of Lethbridge on a farm called Broxburn Vegetables. Broxburn is known for its great veggies, grown almost year-round in greenhouses and all summer in fields. The produce is available at many farmers' markets, and we consume many kilos of their beans, peppers, tomatoes, cucumbers and lettuce at home.

If we're in the Lethbridge area, Broxburn Café is a must-stop. You want fresh? It doesn't get fresher than this. The Broxburn house salad is packed with vegetable goodness and tossed with a lively vinaigrette. (This is perhaps the only restaurant in these parts where I would order the house salad as a main course.)

Of course, I'd start with a bowl of Broxburn's roasted red pepper soup. They use their cosmetically challenged peppers for the soup, those with a bruise or a sunburn or just a gnarly outlook on life. They roast and purée them and serve the soup with a sweet-chili sour cream. (Yes, they grow the chilies.)

Broxburn serves meaty things, too, like chicken salad or steak-and-mushroom sandwiches and chicken sausages with smoked Gouda perogies—simple, tasty stuff. There's even a kids' menu with, say, mac'n'cheese made with cheddar and Gouda. If you visit outside the lunch hours of 11 am and 3 pm, you can still get pie and coffee.

Service is pleasant in a wholesome, on-the-farm way, and the setting is agro-rustic. With a sweeping view of the fields and big bowls of soup and salad inside you, you'll be tempted to pick up a hoe and get to work.

**Address**
5 km east of Lethbridge
on Highway 3 & 1 km south
on Broxburn Road

**Phone**
403.327.0909

**Hours**
May – November:
Monday – Saturday
10 am – 4 pm

December – April:
Tuesday – Saturday
10 am – 4 pm

**Reservations**
Not accepted Saturdays

**Cards**
V, MC, AE, Debit

**Drinks**
Full bar
No corkage

**Outdoor Dining**
Patio

**Noise**
◁)

**Price Range**
$ – $$

**Website**
broxburn-vegetables.com

# Buchanan's

## Chophouse

**S**HOW up at Buchanan's around noon on a weekday, and from the outside, you might not think there's much going on. But step inside and heaven help you if you don't have a reservation. You might get a seat at the bar, but it's unlikely you'll find a free table. They'll all be packed with the downtown office crowd, those who like a good burger or a salmon (red spring) fillet or a roasted pear and candied pecan salad for lunch.

Buchanan's specializes in chophouse cuisine: heavy on the meats and seafood, classic preparations, hearty portions and good service. They've been at it since the late 1980s, so they've got it down to a slick operation.

And it certainly looks the part of a chophouse. There's lots of wood (both on the floor and as room dividers), glass partitions and a long, well-tended bar. Speaking of bars, Buchanan's has the best whisky collection in the city. You want a Scotch? They have over 250 labels here!

But back to that seat at the bar. Aside from being able to gaze longingly at all those whiskies, you're tended to as well as you could possibly want. It's friendly service where you almost feel you can unload your worldly worries on the staff. But don't mistake that for anything less than professional— they'll get the food to you fast (including refills on their fluffy cheese scones) and your drinks even faster.

And then there's that famous bacon cheeseburger, fresh ground and cooked to your preference, a burger appropriate for such a classic chophouse setting.

Just be sure to make a reservation.

**Address**
738 – 3 Avenue SW

**Phone**
403.261.4646

**Hours**
Monday – Friday
11 am – 11 pm

Saturday
5 pm – 11 pm

**Reservations**
Recommended

**Cards**
V, MC, AE, Debit

**Drinks**
Full bar
No corkage

**Outdoor Dining**
Patio

**Noise**
◁) – ◁))

**Price Range**
$$$ – $$$$

**Website**
buchanans.ca

downtown calgary

# Buzzards

## Contemporary Pub

**P**ERHAPS someday there'll be a small historical plaque mounted on the sunny south-facing wall of Buzzards. That would be an appropriate place to honour the first restaurant patio in the city, an innovative idea in the feudal days of 1980. (People sitting outside and drinking? In plain sight of passersby? What folly!)

Yes, someone had to start it, and that someone was Stuart Allan of Buzzards. All the big beer halls of today owe him a nod of thanks and a frothy cool one for convincing the provincial powers that be to let us drink outside. (He's advised the AGLC on other boozy questions, too, like corkage and import regulations.)

All along, Buzzards has been content to be that place just over (or under) the tracks from downtown, the place you go when a chinook hits in February and you want a brew and a burger outside. It just keeps on keeping on.

But Buzzards has never stood still. Allan is taking a less prominent role these days now that son Geoff and daughter Jennifer are running the show. They renovated Buzzards—and Bottlescrew Bill's, the accompanying pub—in 2012, updating the look with contemporary pub tones of dark wood and glass. Meanwhile the menu was contemporized and globalized, too, with Vietnamese-style BBQ pork subs (remarkably tasty), butter-chicken quesadillas, Greek chicken pitas and capicollo wraps. (Note: the big ol' Buzzard Burger remains.)

The food is very respectable—hearty pub fare that doesn't overreach. The biggest issue is what to choose from the list of over 300 beers. And where to hang that plaque.

**Address**
140 – 10 Avenue SW

**Phone**
403.264.6959

**Hours**
Monday – Saturday
11:30 am – 2 am

Sunday
2 pm – midnight

**Reservations**
Accepted

**Cards**
V, MC, AE
ATM

**Drinks**
Full bar
Corkage $10/bottle

**Outdoor Dining**
Large patio

**Noise**
🔊

**Price Range**
$$

**Website**
bottlescrewbill.com

downtown calgary

# Candela

Candela, the second restaurant by Uri Heilik and Rogelio Herrera, is in a far more predictable location than Alloy, their first place. Candela sits on the 4th Street restaurant strip in Mission, occupying a space formerly housed by a Great Canadian Bagel shop, a UPS store and Busy B Cleaners.

The long room, something of a cross between western Mediterranean and sixties hotel lounge, is lit by an immense skylight over a large, central bar. (At night, the skylight acts as a mirror, reflecting the room's activity.) Hand-painted Moroccan tiles cover the floor, and Moroccan-esque lamps hang from the ceiling. Large blue leather-bound chairs surround some tables, and true to the tapas-bar tone, a standing area fronts one side of the bar.

The menu echoes the Mediterranean, but also has global influences. Ranging from scallop ceviche and panko-crusted prawns to chicken tacos and grilled eggplant, the menu is largely made up of small plates for sharing. And though prices have edged up since Candela opened, there's still nothing over $16 on the tapas list. (That's for the Brant Lake Wagyu strip loin with habanero chips.) We find about four tapas are good for the two of us, but choose with care. Some dishes are fried, others are quite fresh and light.

There are some big plates, too, like the lamb shank with Moroccan hummus and chickpea salsa and the roasted chicken with preserved lemon. Those prices are mostly in the mid- to high-$20s.

I like Candela a lot. The combo of food, service and decor helped me tie it with Avec Bistro for top new restaurant in Calgary for 2012.

**Address**
1919 – 4 Street SW

**Phone**
403.719.0049

**Hours**
Monday – Friday
11:30 am – 2 pm

Daily
4 pm – close

**Reservations**
Recommended

**Cards**
V, MC, AE, Debit

**Drinks**
Full bar
Corkage $30/bottle
or bring 1, buy 1

**Outdoor Dining**
None

**Noise**
◁)) – ◁))

**Price Range**
$ – $$$

**Website**
candelalounge.com

# Carino

"Japalian"

**A** GEISHA astride a Vespa. A samurai, sword at the ready, crouched atop a Fiat.

Those are the two graphics on the menu at Carino, a Japanese-Italian bistro at the crest of Edmonton Trail. It's a small place with the big idea of combining Eastern and Western cultures with dishes like a Caprese salad with tofu; Arctic char with polenta and shungiku pesto; and a teriyaki Kobe-style burger. Italian and Japanese flavours mingle with shiso in risotto and yuzu zest on calamari fritters, forcing your palate to embrace a new culinary fusion. Ergo, the Japanese figures on Italian vehicles.

Carino's food is some of the most creative I've seen anywhere lately. The burger is juicy and meaty, a topping of Asian mushrooms and mayo adding layers of remarkably delicate flavour. Delicate for a burger, anyway. They also add a slipperiness, making this one of the messiest burgers I've had. Still, one of the best.

Carino doesn't stop at innovative food. Owner Toshi Karino used to be Teatro's wine director, so he knows his beverages. What goes with a Japanese lamb rib pot au feu or mozzarella agedashi with ume paste? Tricky choices, but Karino has over 60 well-selected wines he will happily and expertly pair with the food.

Carino's setting adds to the unusual nature of the experience. It's small, with 30-odd seats packed into a century-old space. There's a banquette along one wall, a bar in one corner, and you step almost directly off Edmonton Trail into the dining room. There's no waiting area, not even room to park your Vespa or hang your sword.

**Address**
709 Edmonton Trail NE

**Phone**
403.984.7534

**Hours**
Tuesday – Saturday
11 am – 2 pm

Sunday
11 am – 3 pm

Tuesday – Thursday
5 pm – 10 pm

Friday & Saturday
5 pm – 11 pm

Sunday
5 pm – 9 pm

**Reservations**
Recommended

**Cards**
V, MC, Debit

**Drinks**
Full bar
Corkage $15/bottle
Free corkage Tuesdays

**Outdoor Dining**
None

**Noise**
🔊

**Price Range**
$$ – $$$

**Website**
carinobistro.ca

# The Casbah

**Moroccan**

THE Casbah is one beautiful restaurant. Descend into the lower level of the Building Block, pass through the cast iron gate and you're welcomed into the sumptuous atmosphere of Morocco. Eighty seats are cached behind various red Moorish panels and carpets, soft red lights cast a conspiratorial glow over the room and cushioned benches provide low-to-the-ground seating. Your table may be a huge brass platter or a tile mosaic, and the music winding through the air will be both traditional and contemporary Moroccan.

The food leans to the traditional side: harira soup, the spicy chickpea and lentil soup in a saffron- and ginger-flavoured broth; b'stilla of caramelized onions and roast chicken baked in phyllo pastry and topped with icing sugar and cinnamon; and various couscous and tajine dishes. The couscous, tajines and saffron rice dishes are vegetarian but offer the possibility of adding meats. So, for example, you can order a tmar tajine ($19) of stewed root vegetables and chickpeas topped with pecan-stuffed medjool dates and have it as is. Or for another $8, you can add spiced chicken breast kebabs or lamb medallions or other meats.

I tried the couscous chermoula topped with a richly flavoured chermoula sauce of tomato, garlic, chickpeas and herbs ($18) and added grilled house-made beef merguez sausages ($8 more). A lovely dish—loads of vegetables, a sauce just spicy enough and perfectly cooked couscous and sausages.

For the full effect, try the Tour of the Casbah, a three-course meal ($36) or the Tour of Morocco, a five-course feast ($48).

And be sure to enjoy the scenery in this beautiful restaurant.

**Address**
720 – 11 Avenue SW
(Lower Level)

**Phone**
403.265.9800

**Hours**
Daily
5:30 pm – close

**Reservations**
Recommended

**Cards**
V, MC, AE, Debit

**Drinks**
Full bar
Corkage $25/bottle

**Outdoor Dining**
None

**Noise**
🔊

**Price Range**
$$ – $$$$

**Website**
casbahrestaurant.ca

# Cassis Bistro

## French Bistro

**T**HE pairing of Market 17 and Cassis Bistro in Casel Marché, a small European-inspired retail development at the base of a new condo tower, is a brilliant match. Market 17 has an abundance of fine ingredients and Cassis knows how to prepare them. The little bistro (with about 40 seats) attached to the market serves some of the best bistro cuisine in the city.

Owned by Gilles and Andrea Brassart (Gilles hails from Aix-en-Provence, Andrea, from Calgary) and Dominique Moussu (from Brittany), Cassis captures the flavours of France and the spirit of Canadian agriculture. The experienced restaurateurs source the market for Sunworks chicken, Ewe-nique lamb, Broek Pork Acres products and fresh greens to whip into French classics. Beef tartare, goat cheese and cherry tomato salad, steak frites, and chicken liver parfait are among the dishes served with simplicity and skill. Close your eyes, inhale deeply and you'd think you were in France. (In fact, as with Avec Bistro, the food here is better than most I've had in France recently.)

The setting is French bistro, too, with closely spaced tables, banquettes and a small bar up front. It's simple and pure, with an exit leading into the market, light bulbs dangling inside wine bottles, bread served in French gardening pails, Laguiole knives at the ready and staff dressed casually but professionally.

The food is not rushed. It's sculpted and refined, beyond the need of the bistro but well appreciated by the eye as much as the palate. It's lovely. And lively. Fresh, clean flavours, so simple, so good.

**Address**
2505 – 17 Avenue SW
(Casel Marché)

**Phone**
403.262.0036

**Hours**
Tuesday – Sunday
11:30 am – 2 pm

Tuesday – Saturday
5 pm – 10 pm

Sunday
5 pm – 9 pm

**Reservations**
Recommended

**Cards**
V, MC, AE, Debit

**Drinks**
Full bar
No corkage

**Outdoor Dining**
None

**Noise**
◁)) – ◁))

**Price Range**
$$ – $$$$

**Website**
thecassisbistro.ca

# Catch & the Oyster Bar

**W**HEN I'm asked where to find great seafood, one of the first places to pop to mind is Catch & the Oyster Bar. Whether you're looking for good fish'n'chips, a plate of crab cakes, blackened swordfish with hominy grits or a big batch of freshly shucked oysters, one of these two dining rooms can answer the need.

I'm partial to the more casual tone of the main floor Oyster Bar with its long row of booths and zinc-topped bar. It looks like it's been here forever, courtesy of its historic sandstone Imperial Bank building. The East Coast oyster-bar tone fits perfectly with the old building. The menu fits, too: clam chowder, roasted lobster with chili butter, wild salmon with minted pea pesto, oysters Rockefeller. It's thoughtful seafood, not just because they follow Ocean Wise guidelines, but because they prepare it with panache.

Upstairs, the dining room underwent a major makeover in 2011 and resurfaced as a more colourful yet polished restaurant. (It was a tad staid before.) This is where preparations become more complex and prices nudge up a bit—Arctic char with celeriac purée, sweet potato pavé and preserved lemon vinaigrette ($32), for example, or sea bream stuffed with pancetta and herbs and served with tabbouleh and chimichurri ($40).

So if I'm paying, we're dining on the main floor. If someone else is paying, maybe we're going upstairs.

I should also mention that you can take dedicated carnivores here. There is the odd beef or chicken dish on each menu, and I'm told they're done well. I myself have never had them. I stick to the seafood.

**Address**
100 Stephen Avenue SE

**Phone**
403.206.0000

**Hours**
Catch:
Monday – Friday
11:30 am – 2 pm

Monday – Saturday
5 pm – close

Oyster Bar:
Monday – Friday
11:30 am – close

Saturday
5 pm – close

**Reservations**
Highly recommended

**Cards**
V, MC, AE, Debit

**Drinks**
Full bar
No corkage

**Outdoor Dining**
Patio for Oyster Bar

**Noise**
🔊 (Catch)
🔊 – 🔊 (Oyster Bar)

**Price Range**
$$ – $$$$ (Catch)
$$ – $$$ (Oyster Bar)

**Website**
catchrestaurant.ca

downtown
calgary

# Centini

## Modern Italian

**O**F the many restaurants along Stephen Avenue, one of the most understated from the outside is Centini. Tucked into the southeast corner of the Telus Convention Centre, it's easy to miss. Most of that is due to the architecture of the convention centre, which tends to downplay its tenants.

But once inside Centini, the world changes. A warren of rooms flows together to accommodate groups up to 350. (That's for stand-up functions; seated, it's about half that.) An open kitchen fills the centre and is fronted by seats at a kitchen bar.

These are my favourite seats. I like to watch the kitchen activity as the cooks, led by Fabio Centini, create their dishes. Theirs is a bright, well-organized and spotless kitchen where the rich scent of Italian cooking rolls out. It's also where I can see, and lust after, all the dishes that others have ordered.

Centini's food is high end, with top-quality ingredients often priced in the stratosphere. This is expense-account territory with lobster and crab ravioli in a saffron cream going for $32, rack of lamb with prosciutto and Calabrese olives for $54, and Dover sole à la meunière for $52. It's expertly prepared, though, and served with fine linens and tableware.

But don't think Centini is pretentious. It's high tone for sure, but also approachable and surprisingly relaxed. The Business Express Lunch whales out three-course meals—like a prosciutto sandwich with soup and dessert—in the mid-$20s.

That's what we're having if I'm paying. And we'll be sitting at the kitchen bar.

**Address**
160 Stephen Avenue SE

**Phone**
403.269.1600

**Hours**
Monday – Thursday
11 am – 11 pm

Friday
11 am – midnight

Saturday
5 pm – midnight

**Reservations**
Recommended

**Cards**
V, MC, AE, Debit

**Drinks**
Full bar
No corkage

**Outdoor Dining**
None

**Noise**
◁)) – ◁))

**Price Range**
$$$ – $$$$

**Website**
centini.com

downtown calgary

# Charcut

## Roast House

**W**HAT do you say about a chef who can skin a pig's head in under a minute? Impressive parlour trick, for sure, but what does it say about her food?

In the case of Connie DeSousa, the aforementioned head skinner, it shows her knowledge of basic ingredients, her abilities with the pointy end of a knife and her commitment and focus. Ever try to skin a pig's head? In front of a couple hundred people? With a stopwatch on you? That's focus.

And that's what you get at Charcut, run by DeSousa and chef/business partner John Jackson and their respective spouses, Jean Francois Beeroo and Carrie Jackson: a focus on meat in all its glory, from a handmade mortadella that's been cured in that head skin to some braised bison shanks to the best prime-rib sandwich I've ever had. Look away vegans. Sorry to say, Charcut is a meat-lover's paradise.

But don't think Charcut is all about prime cuts of prime beef. Rather, it's about house-made charcuterie and cheaper cuts done well. That, plus a fine Share Burger built to the size you order: more people equals bigger burger. You'll find the odd fish dish and salad, too, but you know why you're here.

The setting matches the culinary theme with an overall black and red tone, an open kitchen that includes a showcase full of meat, a huge butcher-block communal table and washcloths for napkins. So tuck in, enjoy your meat and consider how long it would take you to skin a pig's head.

Note: Look for Charcut to open Charbar in the Simmons Building (in East Village) in early 2015.

**Address**
899 Centre Street S
(Hôtel Le Germain)

**Phone**
403.984.2180

**Hours**
Monday & Tuesday
11 am – 11 pm

Wednesday – Saturday
11 am – 1 am

Sunday
5 pm – 10 pm

**Reservations**
Recommended

**Cards**
V, MC, AE, Debit

**Drinks**
Full bar
Corkage $30/bottle

**Outdoor Dining**
Patio

**Noise**
🔊)) – 🔊))

**Price Range**
$$ – $$$$

**Website**
charcut.com

# Chef's Table

Contemporary French

**I**F you're looking for the chef with the most entries in this book, look no further than Hotel Arts Group's Duncan Ly. He's the executive chef in charge of Raw Bar and Yellow Door, both in Hotel Arts, and Chef's Table in the Kensington Riverside Inn (KRI). Yes, he's that good.

Chef's Table is one of those unknown places; it's inside the KRI, a boutique hotel along Memorial Drive in Kensington. There's a small dining room and a patio that looks out across the Bow. Many people either don't know about it or think it's just for those who are staying there. Those folks are missing out on some extraordinary food.

Chef's Table is a contemporary restaurant that pairs halibut with lentils, sunchokes, salsify, artichokes and capers and combines foie gras with apricot, peach and star anise into one of the silkiest and best foie gras dishes I've ever had.

The food here is as beautiful as it tastes. A vegetarian agnolotti filled with pea purée is topped with firm baby carrots and saffron foam, creating a visual and taste explosion of orange, yellow and green. And then there's a second explosion of flavour from overtones of ginger and preserved lemon. Outstanding!

Even better, also vegetarian and one of the best things in this book, was a small amuse-bouche of summer gazpacho, surprisingly yellow with peppers and tomatoes and topped with a seasoned oil. A light zippiness on the tongue, it had us all near licking the bowl.

So I like chef Ly's food. At any of his restaurants.

**Address**
1126 Memorial Drive NW
(Kensington Riverside Inn)

**Phone**
403.228.4442

**Hours**
Monday – Friday
7 am – 10 am

Saturday & Sunday
8 am – 1 pm

Monday – Saturday
5:30 pm – 9 pm

**Reservations**
Highly recommended

**Cards**
V, MC, AE, Debit

**Drinks**
Full bar
No corkage

**Outdoor Dining**
Patio

**Noise**
🔊 – 🔊

**Price Range**
$$$ – $$$$

**Website**
kensingtonriversideinn.com

# Chez François | French

**W**ITH the wealth of great food options in Canmore these days, it's easy to bypass Chez François in the Econo Lodge on Bow Valley Trail. But it's been one of the most consistent and consistently busy places in the Bow Valley for well over two decades. That's due largely to the endless commitment of owner-operators Jean-François and Sylvie Gouin. They run the place morning, noon and night, serving visitors and locals alike.

Their menu is nothing less than exhaustive. Known for their eggs Benedict (a classic!), they offer six variations on it, including a Swiss cheese, ham and asparagus option and one with spinach, feta and tomato. There are four varieties of French toast: how about banana and hazelnut chocolate with a brown sugar sauce? Add numerous takes on pancakes, waffles, croissants (there's one with duck pâté), and you have a long breakfast list.

Then there's lunch and dinner. There's a distinct French backdrop in dishes such as baked brie with cranberry-apple chutney, coquilles Saint-Jacques, Brome Lake duck with mango-peppercorn sauce and beef bourguignon. The menu, which has become more casual over the years, broadens out with a spicy lamb burger, liver and onions, smoked salmon pasta and a vegan phyllo roll of spinach, chanterelles, pinto beans and cashews. It's, shall we say, eclectic.

It's also, often, very busy. Chez François consumes a couple of large rooms and is a favourite of tour groups. Busy or not, we've never had problems finding a quiet table, good service and fine food.

**Address**
1604 Bow Valley Trail
(Econo Lodge)
Canmore

**Phone**
403.678.6111

**Hours**
Daily
7 am – 2:30 pm

Thursday – Tuesday
4:30 pm – 10 pm

**Reservations**
Recommended

**Cards**
V, MC, AE, Debit

**Drinks**
Full bar
Corkage $15/bottle

**Outdoor Dining**
None

**Noise**
◁ – ◁)

**Price Range**
$$ – $$$

**Website**
restaurantchezfrancois.com

# Cibo

**P**ERHAPS no restaurant epitomizes the increased casualization of dining more than Cibo. When Creative Restaurants opened sister-restaurant Bonterra over a decade ago, it was looked upon as a casual and contemporary alternative to traditional, white-tableclothed Italian restaurants. But now that they have opened the even more casual Cibo, Bonterra looks almost formal in comparison.

Cibo is located in a two-storey brick building erected in the 1930s as a machine shop. More recently, it was a Rogers video store. (How things change.) Cibo's owners stripped the walls back to their Medicine Hat-kilned bricks, and they used recycled wood, including pine beetle-affected pine, to build floors and panel the bar. It has a casual, rustic, open look that generates high volumes of noise. Cibo is definitely not the place for a quiet dinner for two (unless you can snag a spot on the lovely patio).

Cibo is a good place, however, to take a group. Start with scodellini (appetizers) of chicken livers with pancetta, marinated mushrooms with charred chilies, roasted eggplant, walnut salad with Gorgonzola, and build from there. One scodellina is $4, three are $11, five are $18—all set for sharing.

Then move on to salads, pizzas, pastas and such, which are mostly served for sharing. It can be a bit chaotic: the food arrives when it's ready, in whatever order it's been prepared. But dig in, pass it around, share and enjoy.

Because Cibo—albeit loud, lively and chaotic—is always fun and, of course, casual.

**Address**
1012 – 17 Avenue SW

**Phone**
403.984.4755

**Hours**
Daily
11 am – late

**Reservations**
Accepted

**Cards**
V, MC, AE, Debit

**Drinks**
Full bar
Corkage $15/bottle

**Outdoor Dining**
Patio

**Noise**
◁)) – ◁))

**Price Range**
$$ – $$$

**Website**
cibocalgary.com

# Clay Oven | Indian (Punjabi)

SINCE 1997, I've said that Clay Oven serves the best Indian breads in Calgary. Well, my opinion on that remains. Gulijan Sayed, the woman who's made them almost since day one, is still going strong at Clay Oven.

But beyond the breads, Clay Oven serves some of the best Northern Indian food in Calgary—even though the place has (sort of) changed hands. Original owner Gurnek Gill retired in 2009 and passed the tandoori torch to son Preet and staffer Bindu Kandola, both of whom had worked there for years.

Dishes here are still thoughtfully prepared to maximize flavours and textures. Too many Indian dishes seem rushed or short-cut these days; at Clay Oven, the meaty depth of a lamb gosht, the intense spicing of a simple dal and the richness of a true butter-chicken come through. Every dish is a flavour parade that demands your attention. In the roasted eggplant baingan bharta, for instance, your taste buds are first hit with the light acidity of fresh eggplant; next, the spices roll over your tongue; and then, tying it all together, the smokiness hits. Wrapped in a creamy, creamy texture, you almost want to stop chewing and just let it rest in your mouth. It's somehow soothing.

That's because of the quality ingredients—no fatty lamb or bony chicken here. And because they know how to handle those ingredients just so. That's why Clay Oven remains one of the very best Indian restaurants in Calgary.

**Address**
3132 – 26 Street NE
(Interpacific Business Park)

**Phone**
403.250.2161

**Hours**
Monday – Friday
11:30 am – 2 pm

Monday – Thursday
5 pm – 8:45 pm

Friday & Saturday
5 pm – 9:30 pm

**Reservations**
Recommended

**Cards**
V, MC, Debit

**Drinks**
Full bar
Corkage $10/bottle

**Outdoor Dining**
None

**Noise**
◁)

**Price Range**
$$

**Website**
clayovencalgary.com

# Colonial

## Vietnamese Fusion

**W**HEN fire destroyed his Colonial restaurant in Quarry Park, Kenny Nguyen didn't sit around waiting for adjustors and investigators to sort things out. He just opened a second Colonial instead. This one, in the heart of downtown in Art Central across from the Hyatt and the Bow building. (Unfortunately, within months of opening, he received news that Art Central would be demolished, likely in 2015.) While Quarry Park was—and is now again—sleek and modern, Art Central is—or perhaps was, depending on when you're reading this— reminiscent of colonial Southeast Asian hotel bars.

Now that the Quarry Park location is up and running again, we can enjoy Nguyen's food in two spots, at least for a while. Both restaurants prepare an identical menu that provides an upscale spin on Vietnamese classics. Take, for example, the pho. Often a bowl of broth and noodles served for about $6, Colonial's satay seafood pho is packed with scallops, prawns and salmon along with noodles, greens and a broth that dances with flavour. It's also $17, enough to create sticker shock for some. But call it bouillabaisse and serve it in a bistro for $25 and no one would blink an eye.

Colonial also creates unique dishes such as coconut-crusted prawns with a sweet chili-basil sauce and caramelized salmon lacquered in a jalapeno-spiked fish sauce. It's all about flavour, a mix of textures and very pretty plates.

And dessert. Sure, they have the obligatory fried bananas, but they also do a killer crème brûlée—there's that French colonial influence. Try the mango brûlée if they have it. That's true East meets West fusion.

**Address**
917, 163 Quarry Park Boulevard SE

**Phone**
403.460.4097

**Outdoor Dining**
Patio

**Noise**
◁)

---

**Address**
100 – 7 Avenue SW (Art Central)

**Phone**
587.351.6729

**Outdoor Dining**
None

**Noise**
◁) – ◁))

downtown calgary

---

**Common Info**

**Hours**
Monday – Saturday
11 am – 9 pm

**Reservations**
Accepted

**Cards**
V, MC, AE, Debit

**Drinks**
Full bar
Corkage $15/bottle

**Price Range**
$$ – $$$

**Website**
No

# The Coup

**Contemporary Vegetarian**

LATE morning, on the sidewalk of 17th Avenue just west of 8th Street SW, a cluster of people forms. Most are women, some in yoga gear, others garbed for work, all looking a little peckish. Before long, a door opens, a tousle-haired server leans out with a warm welcome and the crowd streams into the Coup. They choose favourite spots—quiet corner booths or sunny, avenue-facing tables—and settle in for a favourite dish.

What is it about the Coup that makes it so popular?

It's not because it's new and trendy. The Coup has been around since 2004, spinning its particular blend of vegetarian and vegan cuisine. Some of the dishes, like the "war and peas" soba noodle salad, have been on the menu since day one.

It's not because the owners follow the "local, seasonal, organic" mantra espoused by so many these days. They do, but there are plenty of places that support local producers and serve organic whenever possible.

I think it's because the Coup has always been true to their ideals. They've always focused on the vegetarian market, accommodated vegans when possible, and hauled out the eggs and cheese when they felt like it. They've never taken reservations, always kept an understated, yet hip, tone to the room and always hired staff that amplified that tone. (Staff uniforms? Hah! T-shirts and snow boots, maybe.)

So the Coup continues to work exceptionally well. It's well conceived and executed, unwavering in its commitment to its seasonal, vegetarian ideals and successful in keeping up with the times.

Note: The Coup's attached Meet lounge offers a short list of Coup snacks.

**Address**
924 – 17 Avenue SW

**Phone**
403.541.1041

**Hours**
Tuesday – Friday
11 am – 3 pm
5 pm – 10 pm

Saturday
9 am – 3 pm
5 pm – 10:30 pm

Sunday
5 pm – 9 pm

**Reservations**
Not accepted

**Cards**
V, MC, Debit

**Drinks**
Full bar
Corkage $20/bottle

**Outdoor Dining**
Small patio

**Noise**
◁) – ◁))

**Price Range**
$$ – $$$

**Website**
thecoup.ca

# Coyotes

Contemporary
Southwestern

**Address**
206 Caribou Street
Banff

**Phone**
403.762.3963

**Hours**
Daily
7:30 am – 10 pm

**Reservations**
Recommended

**Cards**
V, MC, AE, Debit

**Drinks**
Full bar
Corkage $20/bottle

**Outdoor Dining**
2 tables

**Noise**
🔊 – 🔊)

**Price Range**
$ – $$$

**Website**
coyotesbanff.com

**T**HERE's always been an odd juxtaposition of having a Southwestern restaurant with Mediterranean undertones in the mountain shadows of downtown Banff. But since 1993, Coyotes has been packing them in morning, noon and night.

Some come for the corn tortilla and chicken soup, as good as I've had in Santa Fe. Others like the orange-chipotle prawns or the apple-Gorgonzola flatbread with toasted pecans, spinach, mozzarella and goat cheese.

Me, I like breakfast at Coyote's. Theirs is as much about a straight-ahead bacon and egg style as it is about the Southwest or the Mediterranean. Sure, there's a breakfast burrito filled with green chilies, tomatoes, scrambled eggs, chorizo and cheese. Huevos rancheros with blue corn tortillas and red chili sauce pops up, too, as does an artichoke frittata. But many of the dishes are in the range of granola, French toast, smoked salmon scrambled eggs and the Mountain Man of eggs, pancakes, back bacon (or chorizo) and roasted potatoes. I'm fond of the wild-berry buttermilk pancakes, three beautifully cooked pancakes topped with a mix of berries and maple syrup. You can almost feel healthy about such a meal. Until you smear on a few slabs of butter, that is.

Coyotes is a compressed space with a long diner counter and tables squeezed into every available spot. There are a few more tables on the south-facing sidewalk, too, for those occasional hot mountain days. The setting is part diner, part Southwestern and part Banff, and somehow it all works.

Regardless of—or perhaps because of—the odd combination of decor and cuisine, Coyote's has become a Banff classic.

# Crazyweed

Global Fusion

**F**OR years I've touted Crazyweed as one of my all-time favourite restaurants. Chef/owner Jan Hrabec has wowed me with her food for decades, going back to her early days at Joshua's in Banff. And now that daughter Eden and son Wyatt have risen in Crazyweed's culinary ranks, it's great three times over.

Jan won Calgary's Gold Medal Plates competition in 2009, and Eden duplicated the feat in 2012. That in itself is a testament to how talented this family is. I once lost seven minutes of my life to a lamb sandwich created by Jan. And a scamorza cheese and balsamic-roasted tomato pizza once brought tears to my eyes. True stories.

Crazyweed used to reside in the tiny downtown Canmore spot where O Bistro now sits, but moved to their large, slope-roofed place a few years ago. Some people like the lean, clean lines and mountain views. Others, not so much, finding the space too stark and linear. I fall into the first category, and especially like that the drafts of the old place are gone.

And the food! A world-wide collection of Thai grilled chicken; truffled gnocchi with mushrooms, seared scallops and mushy peas; smoked back ribs with a bourbon-mango sauce; salt and pepper calamari. Deeply, intensely layered with flavours, food that silences a table as it commands your attention. Each dish has a unique spin, and vegetarian options, like a creamy polenta with roasted mushrooms, salsa rosa and shaved pecorino, are equal to the rest of the menu.

It's marvelous fare—that's why I'll keep touting Crazyweed.

**Address**
1600 Railway Avenue
Canmore

**Phone**
403.609.2530

**Hours**
Daily
11:30 am – 3 pm
5 pm – 10 pm

**Reservations**
Recommended

**Cards**
V, MC, Debit

**Drinks**
Full bar
No corkage

**Outdoor Dining**
Patio

**Noise**
◁) – ◁))

**Price Range**
$$$ – $$$$

**Website**
crazyweed.ca

# Cucina

Modern Mediterranean

**W**HEN Eighth Avenue Place arrived on the site of the former Penny Lane, I was expecting some sleek, contemporary, stylish restaurant to open there. But Cucina, owned by the same folks who have Teatro and Vendome, looks nothing like the rest of the building.

Cucina is a small, 50-seat, nouveau-rustic bistro with an open kitchen, whitewashed walls, and black and white mosaic tile floors. A tall wine cabinet is fronted by a rolling ladder that allows staff to climb up and retrieve orders. Most tables are zinc-topped, and they are tucked into every available corner. So instead of being open and spacious, it's quite tight, even a bit too tight if all the tables are full.

Cucina rolls from early morning coffee and breakfasts of house-made granola, porchetta-topped Benedicts, and orecchiette pasta frittatas with goat cheese and cherry tomatoes through to lunches of peach and prosciutto salads and elk lasagna. There's even an early "grab & go" option weekdays for those in need of sandwiches and salads (and coffee and pastries on Saturdays).

For dinner (and lunch), they serve a chicken liver parfait with balsamic-braised cipollini onions and sour cherries on house-baked crostini. Both times, ours was outstanding. We've also enjoyed the vitello tonnato, thinly sliced veal strip loin topped with a tuna confit emulsion. And a salad of White Gold burrata mozzarella with tomato and arugula was terrific. Dessert was totally delightful, a citrus trio of lemon pot de crème, lemon cake and lemon-pistachio fudge—all, top-notch.

So Cucina may look like it doesn't belong, but it definitely tastes like it does.

**Address**
515 – 8 Avenue SW
(Eighth Avenue Place)

**Phone**
587.353.6565

**Hours**
Bistro:
Monday – Friday
7 am – close

Saturday
10 am – close

Grab & Go:
Monday – Friday
6:30 am – 4 pm

Saturday
10 am – 4 pm

**Reservations**
Accepted dinner only

**Cards**
V, MC, AE, Debit

**Drinks**
Full bar
Corkage $25/bottle

**Outdoor Dining**
Patio

**Noise**
◁) – ◁))

**Price Range**
$$ – $$$

**Website**
eatcucina.com

**downtown calgary**

# Da Guido

Italian

Consider the menu at Da Guido to be just a suggestion. Sure, there are 14 antipasti, an equal number of pasta dishes and a whole swack of veal, beef, chicken and seafood options. But chef/owner Guido Panara says they're just the tip of the prosciutto. Is there something you'd like that you don't see on the menu? Just ask. That's what over half of his customers do.

Panara says he has a thousand recipes for pasta rolling around in his head. The talented Rome-trained chef has an encyclopedic knowledge of Italian cuisine, and he likes to share it.

Not that there's anything wrong with the menu items. A simple spaghetti carbonara sings with pancetta, Parmesan and egg. The cannelloni Guido of homemade crepes wrapped around veal in a tomato and béchamel sauce is delicate and delightful. There's high quality throughout the fare.

As there is in the setting. Da Guido has been around since 1984, and since 1989, in its current location. Panara built his restaurant not only to showcase his cooking, but also to provide his customers a high level of comfort. So there are two rooms, a central entry and waiting area, carpets on the floors, and linens and crystal glasses on silence-clothed tables. A large wine cellar provides a selection of mostly Italian wines. Servers are decked out in white shirts and black vests.

It's old school and it works. If you're looking for an elegant, well-prepared and expertly served Italian meal, this is the place, on the menu or off.

**Address**
2001 Centre Street N

**Phone**
403.276.1365

**Hours**
Tuesday – Friday
11:30 am – 2 pm

Monday – Saturday
5 pm – close

**Reservations**
Recommended

**Cards**
V, MC, AE, Debit

**Drinks**
Full bar
No corkage

**Outdoor Dining**
None

**Noise**
◁ – ◁))

**Price Range**
$$ – $$$$

**Website**
daguido.ca

# De Thai | Thai

**T**HAI Nongkhai is a Friday-night favourite and a family-event destination for us. It's the good food, nice service, comfortable setting and family-friendly tone that attract us. Run by King and Pern Promcharoenwatana, it's become one of the best Thai restaurants in Calgary. But this page is about De Thai. So why talk about Thai Nongkhai?

Because in addition to running Thai Nongkhai, the couple has taken over the former Rasoi restaurant in Marda Loop and reopened it as De Thai. They retained most of the upscale Southeast Asian look, the butter-soft leather banquette, the textured wallpaper, even the wine racks. They altered the kitchen to accommodate Thai woks, but kept the change simple and quick, opening just a few weeks after taking over.

They brought over the menu from Thai Nongkhai, but with some soft upgrades. They swapped out basa—the go-to fish for many Asian restaurants—and brought in salmon instead. They cranked up the heat in the Crying Tiger beef so that a tiger really would cry. Instead of using large tin pots for the coconut rice, they now serve it in individual bowls and top it with coconut milk. The candied chicken is still crisp yet soft, and the papaya salad still jumps with its chili-spiked dressing. This is great Thai food.

Part of why we like it is also the contemporary look in such things as the plateware and cutlery. The food just looks so good on De Thai's new white plates. And the wine list is short and smart.

Any way we look at it, there are now more choices for Friday nights.

**Address**
101, 2215 – 33 Avenue SW

**Phone**
403.705.2203

**Hours**
Tuesday – Friday
11:30 am – 2 pm

Tuesday – Thursday
5 pm – 9:30 pm

Friday & Saturday
5 pm – 10:30 pm

Sunday
5 pm – 9 pm

**Reservations**
Recommended,
especially weekends

**Cards**
V, MC, Debit

**Drinks**
Full bar
Corkage $12/bottle

**Outdoor Dining**
2 bistro tables

**Noise**
◁ – ◁))

**Price Range**
$$

**Website**
dethaicuisine.com

# Delhi Darbar

**D**RIVING along along 16th Avenue N (the Trans-Canada Highway) with its many and colourful signs, it's easy to miss Delhi Darbar. Tucked in among a bunch of ho-hum joints, it lacks street presence, but it is, after all, more important to concentrate on the traffic. If you pass it by, though, you'll be missing out on a couple of things: one, a tasty list of both traditional and what owner Sanjay Kumar calls fusion dishes; and two, ample free parking out back.

Kumar is a talented young chef who brings flavour by the bucket to his restaurant. You want hot? There's beef Madras done with Southern Indian spices and coconut. Or prawn vindaloo in what Kumar calls a "sense-tingling preparation." Want vegetarian? There's zeera aloo (potatoes cooked with cumin) and dal makhani (black lentils cooked with a special herb blend).

And those fusion dishes? Kumar throws a contemporary spin on a traditional roasted eggplant dish by combining it with butternut squash in a coconut sauce tinged with curry leaves. And he perks up a prawn Malabar dish with a honey-Dijon mustard. Tasty stuff. If that's not enough, Delhi Darbar makes nan stuffed with chopped chicken or ground beef or cream cheese—a different spin on Indian fare than we usually see in these parts.

Delhi Darbar keeps things reasonable, too, with most dishes—even the prawn ones—under $13. Some of the fancy plates are higher, but nothing breaks $16. And for great value, there's also a lunch buffet for $13 (Sunday through Friday) and a dinner buffet for $19 (Monday through Wednesday).

So, don't judge this restaurant by its cover.

**Address**
122 – 16 Avenue NE

**Phone**
403.230.3088

**Hours**
Sunday – Friday
11:30 am – 2 pm

Daily
5 pm – 10 pm

**Reservations**
Accepted

**Cards**
V, MC, AE, Debit

**Drinks**
Full bar
Corkage $10/bottle

**Outdoor Dining**
None

**Noise**
◁))

**Price Range**
$ – $$$

**Website**
delhidarbar.info

# Double Zero

Pizza & Italian

**B**ASEMENT restaurants have a hard time. We don't seem to like descending into a windowless rumpus room for our food. For a drink, maybe. There are only a couple of basement restaurants in this book and not many second storey ones either. (I guess we don't like to climb stairs either.)

Double Zero, the pizza parlour in the Core shopping centre, is one of the lower-level places that actually works. (Note: The entrance is on 4th Street SW.) It works because it has good pizza in an area (downtown) with very little good pizza.

They use finely milled Italian, double-zero flour—ergo, the name—to create thin-crust pizzas. These are topped with San Marzano tomatoes, local mozzarella, and high-grade meats and vegetables. And although you can get a fine margherita pizza, you can also have one topped with spinach and potato or mortadella and pistachios. Or you can go *bianco* with a white sauce, confit chicken, mushrooms and smoked pancetta. You can even have it on a gluten-free crust if you'd like.

Double Zero also does a decent list of pastas, panini and dishes such as roasted steelhead or brick-roasted chicken—chicken that's weighted down by a heavy brick while it's roasting. (So it doesn't fly away? No, to cook it quickly and ensure it's tender.) Double Zero prides itself on a long—and widely priced—wine list as well as some fine beers. What could be better with pizza?

And hey, no sunlight is going to glare in your eyes down here. Look for a second Double Zero, too, in the northeast corner of Chinook Centre in early 2014.

**Address**
751 – 4 Street SW
(In the Core)

**Phone**
403.265.9559

**Hours**
Monday – Friday
11 am – close

Saturday
5 pm – close

**Reservations**
Accepted

**Cards**
V, MC, AE, Debit

**Drinks**
Full bar
No corkage

**Outdoor Dining**
None

**Noise**
◁))

**Price Range**
$$ – $$$

**Website**
doublezeropizza.ca

downtown calgary

# Downtownfood

**Modern Bistro**

**F**OR someone who really lives by the local, seasonal, grown-as-close-to-home-as-possible creed, Darren MacLean still gets around. The menu at his downtown restaurant includes scallop, mussel and tuna ceviche; pappardelle carbonara; and quail tempura with anticucho sauce (anticuchos are a Peruvian specialty most popularly made with beef heart). But even though MacLean's influences are clearly global, his ingredients still come from as close to home as possible, including his roof-top garden (that's pretty darn close to home).

Flavours jump at Downtownfood. The crispy-fried pork cakes are boosted by kimchi, pickled vegetables and a Korean barbecue sauce. The duck confit is wrenched out of France by braised cabbage, Chinese black mushrooms and more of that barbecue sauce. Lively! And it doesn't stop there. A delicate cannoli is brought to life with orange risotto and grapefruit sorbet. It's wacky and it works.

Downtownfood has been a work in progress since opening in early 2012. As it's gained confidence and shifted its look from resto-lounge to restaurant, it's attracted a loyal following for its creativity and intricacy of execution. It's surviving and even thriving in a location that's more challenging than it should be.

Much of that success—perhaps all—is due to the indomitable spirit and talent of MacLean, who hails from Innisfail. He's a local boy who knows his producers, and he knows what to do with their products. He's made Downtownfood into one of those little gems you feel special about after you've discovered it.

**Address**
628 – 8 Avenue SW

**Phone**
587.353.3474

**Hours**
Monday – Thursday
11 am – 10 pm

Friday
11 am – midnight

Saturday
5 pm – midnight

**Reservations**
Recommended

**Cards**
V, MC, AE, Debit

**Drinks**
Full bar
Corkage $25/bottle

**Outdoor Dining**
None

**Noise**
◁))

**Price Range**
$$$

**Website**
downtownfood.ca

# Escoba

Mediterranean
Influenced

**Address**
624 – 8 Avenue SW

**Phone**
403.543.8911

**Hours**
Monday – Friday
11 am – 10 pm

Saturday
5 pm – 10 pm

**Reservations**
Recommended

**Cards**
V, MC, AE, Debit

**Drinks**
Full bar
Corkage $25/bottle

**Outdoor Dining**
None

**Noise**

**Price Range**
$$ – $$$

**Website**
escoba.ca

WHEN Penny Lane, the former brick mall on 8th Avenue, fell to the wrecking ball, the many restaurants inside were scattered to the winds. Some closed forever, while others relocated as close to their old downtown digs as possible. The quickest, and closest, to reopen was Escoba. In a matter of weeks, they were up and running in a larger, more flexible, ground-level space.

The new Escoba seats about 185 over a number of rooms, so it never feels vacuous. Instead, it feels cozy and cloistered—in a good way. There are some windows that bring natural light into the front rooms, but most of Escoba is closed off from the world. Which is reminiscent of their former basement location.

So Escoba is a comfortable place, and it serves comfortable food, too. It's classic and contemporary at the same time: beef tenderloin carpaccio; lamb chops paired with bison short ribs and smashed sweet potatoes; bacon and chorizo flatbread; chicken and scallops with saffron sauce; pavlova with lemon custard. It's hearty food that covers the plate with creativity and care, welcoming food that doesn't intimidate.

Prices don't intimidate either, and the wine list is well chosen for value. The lamb-bison duo tops the menu at $34 (remarkable considering the cost of those two meats), but most entrees stay in the $20s. So though it's not a cheap place, you get the real sense that they want to provide a good meal at a fair price.

And that they won't be moving again anytime soon.

**downtown calgary**

# Farm

**F**ARM opened simultaneously with the arrival of the 2008 recession, but has managed to stay busy ever since. It helps that it's small and comfy and harkens to a Depression-era sensibility—albeit idealized—with its nouveau-farmhouse decor and local-first menu.

Farm looks the part with waist-high wainscotting topped by a salon wall of framed images. An open kitchen fills almost half the space, and about 40 seats are squeezed into the rest. You sit on low wood-and-metal chairs or at a high communal table or at tall seats along the kitchen bar while chowing down on big plates of mac'n'cheese (with Gruyère and aged cheddar) or turkey Cobb salad.

Farm's menus (there are many) are filled with constantly changing dishes that key on market availability. Last time, for example, we had a market salad packed with Lethbridge hothouse arugula and tomatoes, local quinoa and pickled onions, and B.C. walnuts and blue cheese. Nice. Likewise, the Farm sandwich and the vegetables are always in seasonal flux. Meanwhile, some dishes, such as the Arctic char ($24) and the Silver Sage strip steak ($29), remain constants.

The menus: there's one for cheese and charcuterie, one for apps and mains, one for drinks, one for desserts, plus one for daily features. It's a bit complex, but hard to make a bad choice.

Note: Farm doubles as the 17th Avenue presence of Janice Beaton Fine Cheese, which is located in the back and accessed either through a short hallway or off 16th Avenue SW.

**Address**
1006 – 17 Avenue SW

**Phone**
403.245.2276

**Hours**
Monday – Friday
11:30 am – close
(limited menu,
2 pm – 5 pm)

Saturday & Sunday
10:30 am – close
(limited menu,
2 pm – 5 pm)

**Reservations**
Accepted, except for weekend brunch

**Cards**
V, MC, AE, Debit

**Drinks**
Beer & wine
Corkage $15/bottle
Free corkage Mondays

**Outdoor Dining**
Small patio

**Noise**
◁))

**Price Range**
$$ – $$$

**Website**
farm-restaurant.com

# Fine Diner

**Contemporary Canadian Bistro**

**Address**
1420 – 9 Avenue SE

**Phone**
403.234.8885

**Hours**
Daily
7 am – 3 pm

**Reservations**
Accepted Monday – Friday

**Cards**
V, MC, Debit

**Drinks**
Full bar
Corkage $10/bottle

**Outdoor Dining**
None

**Noise**
◁ – ◁))

**Price Range**
$$

**Website**
finedinercalgary.com

FOLLOWING in the chef's clogs of Giuseppe Di Gennaro and his memorable Capo restaurant (read more in the Borgo entry) was a mighty sizable challenge for Rob Greco. So when the chef/owner of Fine Diner took over the empty Capo location, he kept some of the look and all of the kitchen equipment. But instead of trying to replicate high-end Italian cuisine, he went for an upscale diner approach. Smart move, and well in keeping with the Inglewood neighbourhood.

Greco shoehorned in a few more tables, added dimpled steel panels to the kitchen walls to create a diner tone and hired servers who appear to have coffee pots grafted to their hands. So while, on the one hand, the butter-soft leather banquettes elevate the room (and are comfy on the butt), on the other, service adheres to the quick and efficient diner style. More smart moves.

So what is an upscale "fine" diner all about? Well, there's seared ahi tacos with mango salsa and chili-lime aioli; DLTs of duck breast, lettuce and tomato; truffled mac'n'cheese (also available with prosciutto, jalapenos or bacon); and, of course, the requisite breakfast dishes, including duck breast eggs Benedict and banana bread French toast. Is that fine enough?

Fine Diner sources as locally as possible, including from gluten-free bakeries and 15 Kilo Coffee Roasters by Phil & Sebastian (not much coffee grown in these parts, but there *is* darn good roasting). So the quality is always there.

The only downside is frequent weekend lineups. But, once you're in, the experience is mighty fine.

# Flatlands

Prairie Cuisine

**J**ust like Pavlov's dogs, I've been conditioned. Every time I drive by the corner of 11th Avenue and 5th Street SW, I start to salivate. I can't seem to help it. Flatlands is there.

And I'm not alone. I've seen you in there, too, wiping the corner of your mouth. Just try to step into the little café, inhale the aroma of roasting bison and fresh-baked cookies and not salivate.

I like Flatlands—the simplicity of the food, the diligence of the owners, the cheekiness of the name. Owners Brent Robinson and Andrew Blevins have a straightforward approach: up early to whip those omelettes into shape for breakfast regulars and get that bison roasting for lunch sandwiches, shut 'er down by 2 pm, take weekends off. It works, not only for them, but for their throng of fans. And then there's that name. Instead of creating some euphemistic or colourfully overblown moniker, Blevins and Robinson looked east to where the bison used to roam. They took their inspiration from the land around them, which also helps define their food. Flatlands: it's simple, clean and honest. Just like the Prairies.

They're also smart with the food presentation. Those fresh-baked cookies, cinnamon buns, brownies and such are laid out on the counter in full view (and full aroma). Drop in for a quick sandwich to-go or to-stay, and you'll be hard pressed not to add a treat or two. It's OK—we humans are a bit Pavlovian, after all.

**Address**
550 – 11 Avenue SW
(Pattison Square)

**Phone**
403.265.7144

**Hours**
Monday – Friday
7 am – 2 pm

**Reservations**
Accepted, but not necessary

**Cards**
V, MC, AE, Debit

**Drinks**
No alcoholic beverages

**Outdoor Dining**
Small patio

**Noise**
◁ – ◁»

**Price Range**
$

**Website**
flatlandscafe.com

# Fleur de Sel

French Brasserie

RECENTLY, we've seen an influx of French restaurants in Calgary—some very good ones indeed. But I still enjoy the quirky character and brasserie cuisine of Fleur de Sel, established in 1998. It has the charming look and feel of a true French brasserie, down to the baguettes and the mirrored walls.

The soul of Fleur de Sel's character emanates from owner Patrice Durandeau. A consummate saucier, he brings years of experience to the kitchen (when he's cooking) and a saucy attitude to the dining room (when he's serving). When you come to Fleur de Sel, you're in for more than duck pâté and mustard-crusted rack of lamb. You'll be served some attitude, too, so be prepared. Just go with it. (Check out the bathrooms and see what I mean.)

You'll be squeezed into a seat somewhere, perhaps in a place where you might not think there's room. Fleur de Sel is compressed, which makes it easy to meet your neighbours and enjoy the energy. It also makes it a bit tricky for the servers to manoeuvre, so try to minimize grand hand gestures. You may end up poking someone or knocking a scalding onion soup off a tray.

I'm fond of Fleur de Sel's choucroûte of sauerkraut packed with sausages and chops, and the cassoulet with duck confit. But the mussels in a creamy mustard sauce are outstanding, plus the steaks and lamb are always lovely. Even the salads are a treat.

It's all enhanced by Fleur de Sel's unique character. *Bon appétit!*

**Address**
2015 – 4 Street SW

**Phone**
403.228.9764

**Hours**
Tuesday – Friday
11 am – close

Saturday – Monday
5 pm – close

**Reservations**
Recommended

**Cards**
V, MC, AE, Debit

**Drinks**
Full bar
Corkage $15/bottle

**Outdoor Dining**
None

**Noise**
◁))

**Price Range**
$$ – $$$

**Website**
fleurdeselbrasserie.com

# 4th Spot

**F**OR decades Karouzo's—a family-run operation that served big, thick Greek pizzas—was one of the top pizza joints in town. But things change, and in 2011, Karouzo's became 4th Spot Kitchen & Bar. The new owners did a big reno on the place, opening it up, installing new wood floors and a bunch of television screens, converting the upstairs lounge into a second dining room and launching it as a new neighbourhood pub and restaurant.

They kept the family-oriented tone, though, and honoured the history by including a list of Karouzo's pizzas along with a photo of Louis Karouzo himself on the menu. Nice touch.

But 4th Spot also created their own menu of pastas, sandwiches, salads and a second list of pizzas, this one with thinner crusts and eclectic toppings. For example, they have the Bruce Lee pizza with teriyaki-sauced chicken, red onion, pineapple and sesame seeds. These are good pizzas: nice crusts, good sauce, quality toppings and, on Mondays, they're half price.

While Catherine enjoyed her margherita pizza, I went for the meat loaf, two huge slabs covered in thick gravy and sided with warm potato salad, coleslaw and a pile of fresh carrots and broccolini. I thought I was hungry, but I couldn't finish. Great meat loaf and a nice casual evening.

We found 4th Spot left us with a lingering envy that there isn't something quite like it closer to where we live. It's a fine neighbourhood place that's very current, but also honours the past. We don't see enough of those.

**Address**
2620 – 4 Street NW

**Phone**
403.984.3474

**Hours**
Monday – Thursday
11 am – 11 pm

Friday & Saturday
11 am – midnight

Sunday
11 am – 10 pm

**Reservations**
Not accepted

**Cards**
V, MC, AE, Debit

**Drinks**
Full bar
No corkage

**Outdoor Dining**
Patio

**Noise**
◁) – ◁))

**Price Range**
$ – $$

**Website**
4thspot.ca

# Gaucho

## Brazilian BBQ

I F you're looking for a meat fix (vegan alert: look away now!), there are few better destinations than a churrascaria. In these Brazilian barbecue shrines, huge hunks of meat are laced with salt and spit-roasted on a huge rotisserie.

Ede Rodrigues, the owner of these two Gaucho locations, hails from Rio Grande do Sul in southern Brazil where he trained as a churrasco chef. He does the full rodizio service style here where, for a set cost of $37 for dinner or $22 for lunch, the roasted meats are lugged out to you on their spits and carved at your table. And we're not talking about a couple of meats here. Nope. We're talking 13 at dinner, 7 at lunch! From chicken wings and sausages to top sirloin and pork loin, they're served hot and sizzling onto your plate. It's sooooo tasty that way, and even the rump steak is richly flavoured and remarkably tender. (For $14 at lunch, you can order your meal non-rodizio style if you prefer.)

A rodizio-style meal here includes a huge buffet with Brazilian dishes such as feijoada (a national bean dish) and farofa (a toasted manioc flour mixture) for the full effect. To go along with such a feast, you're given a little cardboard cow that's red on one side, green on the other. Just in case all that meat renders you incapable of speech, flip the cow to red-side-up and they'll stop serving you. Green and they keep on coming.

Now that's a meat fix.

**Address**
5920 Macleod Trail S

**Phone**
403.454.9119

**Hours**
Monday – Friday
11 am – 4 pm

Saturday & Sunday
Noon – 4 pm

Daily
5 pm – 10 pm

---

**Address**
629 Main Street
Canmore

**Phone**
403.678.9886

**Hours**
Call for seasonal hours

**Outdoor Dining**
Patio

---

**Common Info**

**Reservations**
Recommended

**Cards**
V, MC, AE, JCB, Debit

**Drinks**
Full bar
Corkage $18/bottle
Free corkage Mondays

**Noise**
◁)

**Price Range**
$$ – $$$

**Website**
brazilianbbq.ca

# Globefish

Sushi & Izakaya

I USED to be a big fan of the small 14th Street NW Globefish (the one that's now Muku). Then the owners opened another in Marda Loop, then another in Chinook and, finally, they shifted the 14th Street restaurant to a larger building next door. So now my biggest issue is deciding which one to visit when I need a sushi fix.

Globefish has a fairly fluid approach to staffing. The sushi cutters move around the three locations, so it's hard to choose one over the other for quality. There are dozens of unique cuts here, some draped over driftwood and "smoking" on dry ice, others sitting over mounds of flaming salt. Your typical sushi, this is not. The "special roll" list reads like a manga comic: God of Fire, Power of Love, Cherry Blossom, Crazy Buster, even an Iginla roll. (Wonder if that one will change?) These are creative combinations. The Crazy Buster, a favourite of mine, starts with tuna and salmon deep-fried into tempura, then rolled with more tuna and drizzled with a spicy mayonnaise—it's crunchy, tangy, and (good) fishy all at the same time.

Each Globefish serves the same menu and has a similar feel. All are lively, there can be lineups and tables are tightly spaced. The Chinook location is close to shopping and has easy access off Macleod Trail, Marda Loop on 33rd Avenue has the best parking and 14th Street is the biggest. Decisions, decisions…

I'm happy at any one of them. The overall quality and creativity make the decision-making process worthwhile.

**Address**
332 – 14 Street NW

**Phone**
403.521.0222

**Reservations**
Accepted for groups
of 6 or more

---

**Address**
6455 Macleod Trail S
(Chinook Centre)

**Phone**
403.457.1500

**Reservations**
Not accepted

---

**Address**
2009 – 33 Avenue SW

**Phone**
403.249.8866

**Reservations**
Not accepted

---

**Common Info**

**Hours**
Contact specific location

**Cards**
V, MC, Debit

**Drinks**
Full bar
Corkage $15/bottle

**Noise**
◁))

**Price Range**
$$

**Website**
globefish.ca

# Glory of India

Indian

**B**ACK in 2002 when Glory of India opened, there wasn't much Indian food in the downtown core. Hard to believe now, I know. Glory set the standard for downtown Indian lunch buffets: it was long, it was richly flavoured and it was a bit more expensive than the buffets outside downtown. Almost immediately there were weekday lineups out the door as the downtown office crowd took to the flavours. And in this high-rent district, few seemed to mind the prices.

Flash forward to 2013 and Glory is still going strong in spite of the arrival of many more Indian restaurants in the area. The lunch buffet is still popular (and pricier at $18) and always tempting.

I prefer the evenings, though, when the daytime crowds are gone and I can order off the menu. (You can do so during lunch, too, but that buffet always looks so good.) In the evening, the Glory experience is amped up. The tandoori dishes are served on smoking, sizzling platters that spew magnificent flavours as well as smoke. The prawn jalfrezi ($21) bites back with intense chili and spices, and the chicken Chatinard ($17), cooked with roasted South Indian spices, tamarind paste, ginger and garlic, gives your taste buds a sublime workout. Glory's menu is long and lush and includes numerous vegetarian dishes such as roasted eggplant (baingan bharta) and chickpeas cooked in mango powder (Pindi chole).

I like to order a bunch of dishes and arrange them on the table, making my own private buffet. No lineups there.

**Address**
515 – 4 Avenue SW

**Phone**
403.263.8804

**Hours**
Monday – Friday
11:30 am – 2 pm

Monday – Saturday
5 pm – 10 pm

**Reservations**
Recommended

**Cards**
V, MC, AE, Debit

**Drinks**
Full bar
Corkage $13.95/bottle

**Outdoor Dining**
Patio

**Noise**
◁ – ◁))

**Price Range**
$$ – $$$

**Website**
gloryofindia.com

downtown calgary

# Grumans

Jewish-Inspired
Delicatessen

**Address**
230 – 11 Avenue SE

**Phone**
403.261.9003

**Hours**
Monday – Friday
11 am – 3:30 pm

Saturday & Sunday
9 am – 3:30 pm

**Reservations**
Not accepted

**Cards**
V, MC, AE, Debit

**Drinks**
Beer & wine
Corkage $15/bottle

**Outdoor Dining**
None

**Noise**
◁ – ◁))

**Price Range**
$$

**Website**
grumans.ca

**A**MONG diehard Montrealers, the debate over smoked meat continues—it's right up there with the fate of the Habs and tributes to the bygone days of Rusty Staub and the rest of *Les Expos*. Sovereignty? Phah! Let's get going on serious topics like whether Schwartz's or Dunn's has the best smoked meat. And what pickle should be served with it.

At Grumans, owner Peter Fraiberg carries a hearty brined style of smoked meat to satisfy his smoked meat fans. He steams it, slices it and piles it high on rye bread, creating a warm, moist, mustard-tinged sandwich that answers the need when cravings arise. You get potato salad or fries with that, along with a pickle—a Putter's brined pickle, to be exact—making it a well-balanced meal of the important food groups (at least that's what my Hab-loving friends tell me, and I tend to agree).

If smoked meat isn't calling you, you can indulge in potato knishes, chopped chicken liver, lox, a tuna melt or even a spinach salad. On Fridays, you can order Bubby's Favourite, slow-roasted brisket. Grumans isn't kosher—there's bacon on the cheeseburger—but it does hew to a good Montreal-style delicatessen.

That's thanks to Fraiberg, a Montreal expat who has channelled his mother's recipes into a menu that pleases. And he's found a setting that works—a blockish, 55-year-old concrete building in the Beltline. It looks like it's been there for a long time and will likely go on forever. Just like the argument over smoked meat.

# The Himalayan

Nepalese

**D**ON'T you just love a great momo? Or a plate of lamb choyla? Or a chicken chatpat? Or a vegetable tarkari? If you know these dishes, you've likely been to Nepal or the Himalayan restaurant in Killarney. (For those who haven't been to either, a momo is a Nepalese dumpling; choyla is grilled meat spiked with garlic, ginger and mustard oil; a chatpat is a stew-like dish with a hot and sour base; and a tarkari is a Nepalese curry. Now don't you just want some?)

The Himalayan, Calgary's only outpost of Nepalese cuisine and one of the few in Canada, features all these dishes and more, like the Mango Fruity with either roasted chicken or shrimp in a mango-tomato-cashew sauce. The food of Nepal is strongly influenced by its two huge neighbours—India and China—so you'll find dishes and flavours reminiscent of both cultures. But you'll find unique Nepalese character, too. Nepalese herbs, and that mustard oil, add a distinct flavour to the dishes.

An essential choice at the Himalayan is the sweet bread. (No, not sweetbreads.) It's a baked nan filled with a sweet coconut concoction, a perfect foil for some of the pungent mustard-oil dishes and practically a meal on its own. Lovely.

Perhaps the best way to try the Himalayan the first time is to go for the lunch buffet. You can sample a broad range of items, figure out which ones you like best (some of the mustard-oil ones can be a bit daunting) and then come back later for dinner. It's like Everest. One step at a time.

**Address**
3218 – 17 Avenue SW

**Phone**
403.984.3384

**Hours**
Tuesday – Saturday
11:30 am – 2 pm

Sunday
Noon – 2 pm

Tuesday – Thursday, Sunday
5 pm – 9 pm

Friday & Saturday
5 pm – 10 pm

**Reservations**
Highly recommended

**Cards**
V, MC, AE, Debit

**Drinks**
Full bar
Corkage $20/bottle

**Outdoor Dining**
None

**Noise**
◁ – ◁))

**Price Range**
$ – $$$

**Website**
himalayancuisine.ca

# Home

**I** WONDER what the Ashdown family would think if they saw their old hardware store these days. The 1891-built sandstone structure served as a hardware store for over 80 years, but in 2010, it was restored and transformed into a restaurant called Home Tasting Room. The restoration uncovered the original wood floors, mosaic tile highlights and sandstone walls, and it's now one of the prettier restaurants along Stephen Avenue.

Home does the "sharing plates" popular in many contemporary restaurants these days. You can order a bunch of them for your group (or yourself) or opt for a dinner or lunch plate of your own. On the sharing side, for example, you might find a grilled Belgian endive salad with bacon, honeycomb and a lovely nutmeg cream ($14.50) or bison tartare ($17.50) or chive and ricotta gnocchi ($15). An abbreviated sharing-plate menu is available mid-afternoons. On the full meal side, you might find a dinner of lamb sirloin with beluga lentils, carrots, spinach and rosemary jus ($28) or a lunch of a confit chicken salad sandwich with bacon and mustard cream ($15). I say "might find" because Home's menu changes seasonally. Regardless, either sharing or ordering my own plate, Home works for me—this is food that keys on natural flavours, beautifully melded.

Presentation is always superb—the dishes are almost too pretty to eat. But in keeping with the name, they also have a homespun tone, what with their own pickled vegetables, canned fruit and charcuterie. They even do their own potato chips and churn their own ice cream.

I think the Ashdowns would like that.

**Address**
110 Stephen Avenue SW

**Phone**
403.262.8100

**Hours**
Monday – Thursday
11 am – 10 pm

Friday
11 am – 11 pm

Saturday
Noon – 11 pm

**Reservations**
Recommended

**Cards**
V, MC, AE, Debit

**Drinks**
Full bar
Corkage $25/bottle

**Outdoor Dining**
Patio

**Noise**
◁) – ◁))

**Price Range**
$$$

**Website**
hometastingroom.ca

downtown
calgary

# Il Centro

I REMEMBER when Il Centro was a hidden gem. Now every time I walk in, there's a huge party going on. And try to get in without a reservation? Fugidaboudid.

It's not any easier to find than it used to be, though, what with its location on the out-of-the-way intersection of 3rd Street and 2nd Street SW. But lately, pizza purists have taken a shine to Fedele Ricioppo's pizza, to its aged, medium-thick crust, its light coating of sauce and its generous toppings. Of the classic, Roman-style pizzas around town, it is among the best, if not THE best.

We almost always start with Il Centro's calamari. Thick rings of calamari are deep-fried with a light crust and then coated with a spicy tomato glaze. Next, while others may opt for the Caesar salad or the gnocchi, a pasta or even a steak, I feel obliged to have a pizza topped with pancetta and mushrooms.

Why? Because it's named after me. It should actually be named after Catherine. She's been a fan of that combo for years, and when we started asking for it at Il Centro, they liked it too. It wasn't very long before it appeared on the menu under my name. (Ask for the pancetta to be thin and crispy.)

There are many other fine pizzas, too, baked medium-sized (mid-teens, dollar-wise) and large (mid-$20s). Not cheap, but these are premium pies. A large always leaves us a couple of slices for breakfast the next day.

So make a reservation, program the GPS and join the party.

**Address**
6036 – 3 Street SW

**Phone**
403.258.2294

**Hours**
Monday – Wednesday
11 am – 2 pm

Thursday – Saturday
11 am – 10 pm

(Closed in August)

**Reservations**
Highly recommended

**Cards**
V, MC, Debit

**Drinks**
Full bar
Corkage $15/bottle

**Outdoor Dining**
None

**Noise**
◁))

**Price Range**
$$ – $$$

**Website**
ilcentropizzeria.ca

# Il Sogno | Italian Influenced

I<small>T</small>'s little things that set Il Sogno apart from run-of-the-mill Italian places. Things like crisp linens (yes, they have tablecloths, an increasingly rare commodity), Royal Doulton china and hand-polished glassware. Owner Patricia Koyich and her staff take the restaurant business seriously and pay attention to even the smallest detail.

Like the butter. It's soft and hand-compounded with seasonings like rosemary and garlic. Tired of ripping good bread apart with cold butter? You'll find no such bread crime, or any other, at Il Sogno.

I appreciate an amuse-bouche, such as a small mound of delicately minted watermelon, on a silver spoon. Food really does taste better on good cutlery.

And with a good glass of wine. Il Sogno's wine list is smart—it focuses on Italian vino, but has global entries, too. There are good bottles in the $40 to $50 range (reasonable these days) and premium selections that creep into the hundreds.

As for food, it's a blend of classic Italian (risotto, Caprese salad, osso bucco) with contemporary overtones (seared scallops and pork belly with fennel purée, duck breast with carrot-maple emulsion, octopus and prawn soup flavoured with saffron). Creative ideas, intelligent preparation.

The house-rolled fusilli (wow!) with house-made Italian sausage, caramelized onion and crème fraîche is a delightful pasta dish. I like that each ingredient—there are only four after all—has a presence. No skimping on the crème fraîche or the onions. Lots of lightly seasoned sausage. Tasty but not overpowering, so the onions and crème come through. And rolling their own fusilli?

Like I say, it's the little things.

**Address**
24 – 4 Street NE

**Phone**
403.232.8901

**Hours**
Monday – Friday
11:30 am – 2 pm

Monday – Saturday
5 pm – 9:30 pm

**Reservations**
Recommended

**Cards**
V, MC, AE, Debit

**Drinks**
Full bar
Corkage $25/bottle

**Outdoor Dining**
None

**Noise**
◁))

**Price Range**
$$ – $$$$

**Website**
ilsogno.org

# Inti

**H**AD a good lomo saltado lately? Or a tasty papa a la Huancaina? We're talking Peruvian cuisine here, one of the hot trends on the culinary scene lately.

Peruvian is a cuisine based partly on the potato—legit seeing as the potato was born in Peru. The papa dish mentioned above is Inti's deconstructed potato salad, made of thick potato slices in a creamy, cheesy, mayonnaisy sauce. Too saucy for you? Try their french fries, some of the best around. These folks know spuds.

There are other interesting things, too. That lomo saltado is a dish of stir-fried beef seasoned with aji amarillo chilies and served over fried potatoes. (See? More potatoes.) There's ceviche done with lime-cured red snapper and two kinds of corn. And there's the intriguing rotisserie chickens made with herbs that only grow in Peru and only above 3,000 metres.

If you can't decide, don't worry. Chef/owner Hans Puccinelli lays them all out—plus many more—on a lunch and dinner buffet. He feels it's the best way to expose Calgarians to Peruvian cuisine: put out a spread and let people sample. Works for him; works for us, too. He's a skilled chef and knows to refill the buffet frequently with small quantities to keep things fresh. (You can fill up on the buffet to-go or to-stay, or order a few things off a short menu, like a sandwich of chicharrón with salsa, sweet potato and avocado mayo.)

It all works for the Incan sun god Inti, too. A mural of the scowling Inti looks down on the buffet as he keeps an eye on the proceedings. I'm thinking he'd like some lomo saltado.

**Address**
3132 – 26 Street NE
(Interpacific Business Park)

**Phone**
587.352.5599

**Hours**
Monday – Saturday
11:30 am – 2 pm
5 pm – 9 pm

Sunday
Noon – 2 pm
5 pm – 8 pm

**Reservations**
Accepted

**Cards**
V, MC, Debit

**Drinks**
Beer, wine & pisco drinks
No corkage

**Outdoor Dining**
None

**Noise**
◁ – ◁୬

**Price Range**
$$

**Website**
inti-restaurant.com

# Jaipur

Indian (Jaipur)

**Address**
114 – 3 Avenue W
Cochrane

**Phone**
403.981.9988

**Hours**
Monday – Friday
11 am – 2 pm

Monday – Saturday
4 pm – close

**Reservations**
Recommended

**Cards**
V, MC, AE, Debit

**Drinks**
Full bar
Corkage $5/bottle

**Outdoor Dining**
Patio

**Noise**
◁ – ◁)

**Price Range**
$$ – $$$

**Website**
jaipurindiacuisine.com

THE history of Cochrane's Jaipur India Cuisine goes back to the early 1970s when Rome and Sue Anand opened Omar Khayyam, one of Calgary's first Indian restaurants. They ran it for years while also raising sons Tony and Rick, and eventually they moved on to open Rajdoot. After a long while, they retired, but then they unretired long enough to help Tony and his wife Raju open Jaipur.

Jaipur is a small house on a Cochrane side street, a cluster of rooms done in rich reds and woody browns with Indian tapestries and weighty bronze ornamentation throughout. It's a calm, casual place that's small enough to quickly fill with the robust scent of Indian food.

The fare here keys around the dishes eaten by the royalty of Jaipur. So there are dishes with fine ingredients like the chicken tikka korma (boneless chicken breast simmered in a cashew sauce), basmati rice biryanis and spice-marinated paneer sautéed with crushed spinach and fenugreek. In keeping with the size of the place (it's only 28 seats), the menu is fairly short, but many additional dishes such as rogan josh, bhuna masala and vindaloos can be prepared if you call ahead.

The Anands' food has always been deep in flavour, and there's no exception here. The platters exude quality throughout, with house-blended spice mixes and less oil and ghee than we often see.

And always, there is a warm welcome. Anand restaurants have consistently conveyed a sense that you're being invited into someone's home. And now it's the home of the next generation, still with occasional visits from Rome and Sue, the elders of the family.

# Jonas' Restaurant

**Hungarian**

**E**VERY once in a while, Catherine gets a craving for chicken paprikash. That leaves us two choices—either fly to Budapest or head downtown to Jonas' Restaurant.

Sure, it would be nice to dip our toes in the Danube, but the Bow is just as nice and so is the welcome at Jonas'. So almost every time, we opt for Jonas'. Rosza Jonas (chef Janos Jonas' wife) is one of the warmest and most skilled restaurateurs in the city. Not that you want to mess with her. If she says you need a bowl of goulash, you need a bowl of goulash. You'll love the intensely flavoured soup-stew.

Just make sure to leave room for the chicken paprikash. Unless you happen to be there on a Tuesday when the special is chicken liver, Hungarian-style—another of Catherine's favourites. I'm partial to Thursdays when the special is creamed lentils and roasted sausage.

If you're a newbie to Jonas', you'll notice that most dishes come in small and regular sizes. Unless you're exceedingly hungry or a Hungarian weightlifter, order the small portion. It will almost feed a couple of people. The regular size can handle a family of four—with leftovers. But the food is so good, you may be able to hoover down a regular-sized order all by yourself. (I've done it once or twice, but have learned better from my actions.)

And don't forget the wine, all Hungarian. It's the perfect match for the food, especially the Tokaji Aszu (sweet at 5 puttonyos!) with the palacsintas (dessert crepes).

**Address**
937 – 6 Avenue SW

**Phone**
403.262.3302

**Hours**
Tuesday – Friday
11:30 am – 2 pm

Tuesday – Saturday
5 pm – 9 pm

**Reservations**
Recommended

**Cards**
V, MC, AE, Debit

**Drinks**
Full bar
Corkage $10/bottle

**Outdoor Dining**
None

**Noise**
◁ – ◁))

**Price Range**
$ – $$$

**Website**
jonasrestaurant.homestead.com

downtown calgary

# Juree's | Thai

THERE used to be a great little Thai place in a northeast hotel called, plainly enough, Thai Place. It became so popular, a second location in the northwest was opened. That one was dubbed Thai Place West and the original was renamed Thai Place East. But in 2011, owner Juree Trentham consolidated both into a new spot called Juree's Thai Place.

Before Juree moved in, the place was a Burger King and it still has some vestiges of its former royalty. A few regal signs remain, as does the drive-through lane, though there's no service at it. (Juree does takeout, but you have to get out of your vehicle and go inside to pick it up.) Otherwise, though, the burger joint has been transformed into a Thai grotto with verdant gardens painted on the walls, water features around the room and lots of plants. It's peaceful and comfortable and very relaxing.

Juree offers a lunch buffet Wednesday to Friday as well as a lengthy menu of Thai favourites on tap at both lunch and dinner. Her tom yum kung (hot and sour prawn soup) grabs your taste buds and won't let go. Kaffir lime leaves, chilies, galangal, lemon grass, lime juice and green onion all ramble around your palate, washing it with fresh, zippy flavours. (I love it, though its chilies can make me cough.) The panang curry adds more chilies and coconut milk to the mix, further tantalizing your mouth. And a simple seafood dish seasoned with basil provides a soothing balance to your meal.

So in my books, Juree's is a great place for Thai food—easily as good as her two Thai Places.

**Address**
2055 – 16 Avenue NW

**Phone**
403.264.6477

**Hours**
Daily
11 am – 10 pm

**Reservations**
Accepted

**Cards**
V, MC, AE, Debit

**Drinks**
Full bar
Corkage $10/bottle

**Outdoor Dining**
None

**Noise**
◁))

**Price Range**
$$

**Website**
thaiplacegroups.com

# Khao San

Thai

**S**OME restaurants seem to last forever, while others come and go. Many of us were sorry to see Jaroblue shuffle off; it was a grand, stylish tapas bar with great food and a striking atmosphere. But it's gone.

In its place, Khao San has opened. To their credit, the new owners kept all the decor—except the horses. Jaroblue had showcased huge photo murals of Sable Island's feral horses, but those left with the owners. Now where once horses ran free, golden dragons frolic. (That's more than a colourful metaphor; Thai tapestries adorned with gold-embroidered dragons now fill the walls.)

And the smell of Thai cooking fills the air. Owners Samphan Treeyachat and Rungroj Suntiwan both hail from northeastern Thailand, so the food leans in that direction as well.

But Khao San is the first Thai restaurant in Calgary to regularly offer khao soi, a hearty noodle-soup-stew dish from the area around Chiang Mai. (Khao soi means "cut rice," indicating the rice flour used to make the noodles.) Khao soi is the lunch dish of choice in Chiang Mai, and many restaurants there serve only that. At Khao San, the khao soi is packed with noodles, chicken and coconut milk and flavoured with yellow curry, lime, shallots and pickled cabbage. It has an amazing range of flavours and textures. And that's just one dish at Khao San.

They offer many other dishes, too, each handcrafted with big Thai flavours. Want heat? They'll do that. Vegetarian? No problem. Soups, salads, curries? You bet. Under the watchful eyes of the dragons, Khao San is an honourable replacement for Jaroblue.

**Address**
1314 – 17 Avenue SW

**Phone**
587.353.2668

**Hours**
Tuesday – Friday
11:30 am – 2 pm

Tuesday – Thursday
5 pm – 9:30 pm

Friday & Saturday
5 pm – 10:30 pm

Sunday
Noon – 9 pm

**Reservations**
Accepted

**Cards**
V, MC, AE, Debit

**Drinks**
Full bar
Corkage $15/bottle

**Outdoor Dining**
Small patio

**Noise**
◁ – ◁)

**Price Range**
$$ – $$$

**Website**
khaosanthaikitchen.ca

# Kinjo

I USED to think there wasn't a wackier, livelier, more crowded and fun restaurant in town than Kinjo on Macleod Trail. Every time I'd go, customers would be crammed around the oval boat bar and staff would be singing songs for birthday parties or family dinners or just because it was time to sing. Plates of free sushi would appear out of nowhere, and in the izakaya style, food and sake flowed. Peter Kinjo himself would wield his big fish knife and pass out boxes of Pocky to anyone who'd take them.

So yeah, I used to think there wasn't a wackier place, until Kinjo opened an even bigger and busier Kinjo in Dalhousie. This new Kinjo is even more madcap, with more tables, more customers, more singing staff, more sushi and even more Pocky. Then a third Kinjo, even spiffier and shinier, opened in Millrise. The only downside is there's only one Peter Kinjo, and the lights are always brighter and the sushi and such tastier when he's around.

Kinjo—the man—is an unstoppable force of hospitality. He directs traffic, he entertains, he leads the singing and he hands out the Pocky. And somehow, he and his staff still make pretty good sushi. It's always fresh; it really has to be, considering the amount they go through.

Service is always crisp, too, even when the joints are packed. General manager and partner Yukiko Kaizuka keeps her smiling servers moving but still having a good time.

There's nothing quite like the Kinjo experience. Quiet and subdued, it is not. But go and have some fun. And a bit of sushi, too.

**Address**
7101 Macleod Trail S

**Phone**
403.255.8998

**Address**
415, 5005 Dalhousie Drive NW

**Phone**
403.452.8389

**Address**
4000, 150 Millrise Boulevard SW

**Phone**
403.452.6888

**Common Info**

**Hours**
Daily
11 am – 10 pm

**Reservations**
Not accepted

**Cards**
V, MC, AE, Debit
ATM

**Drinks**
Full bar
Corkage $12.50/bottle

**Outdoor Dining**
None

**Noise**
🔉 – 🔊

**Price Range**
$ – $$

**Website**
kinjosushiandgrill.com

# Kuzina | Greek Inspired

I DON'T normally think of Greek restaurants for quick business-lunch options. Languid evenings resplendent with souvlakia, horiatiki, hummus, pitchers of retsina and glasses of ouzo, yes. A quick midday in and out, not so much.

But Kuzina, the Greek-inspired restaurant on 17th Avenue, has a three-course business-lunch special priced for the year. (In 2013, for example, it was $20.13.) You choose an appetizer from a list of eleven choices, a main from a list of five and dessert from a list of six. Most of the selections appear on the regular menu; for this, though, they're presented in slightly downsized portions.

I opted for calamari, lamb souvlaki in a pita and galaktoboureko. The calamari came out hot and fast, about a dozen or so rings with a big ramekin of tzatziki. Nice calamari, crisp on the outside, soft inside. Then the pita with a half-dozen large chunks of tender lamb folded into a warm, soft pita with tomato, cucumber, onions, parsley and more tzatziki. (In the regular order, you get double the meat.) Terrific pita, but one note on the tzatziki and the garlic therein: it's delicately applied, but may be contraindicated for an up close and personal afternoon. Finally, the galaktoboureko: creamy custard-filled phyllo. Again, nicely done.

Kuzina is owned by the same family who had Athens by Night in this space. They've updated the look with light, bright, airy tones. And in the evening, they broaden the menu to include contemporary, Greek-inspired dishes like a watermelon-feta-arugula salad and pulled lamb with peas and spinach—food that may require a more languid approach than a quick business lunch.

**Address**
1137–17 Avenue SW

**Phone**
403.245.0060

**Hours**
Sunday & Monday
11 am – 10 pm

Tuesday – Thursday
11 am – 11 pm

Friday & Saturday
11 am – midnight

**Reservations**
Recommended

**Cards**
V, MC, AE, Debit

**Drinks**
Full bar
Corkage $25/bottle

**Outdoor Dining**
Patio

**Noise**
◁) – ◁))

**Price Range**
$ – $$$

**Website**
kuzina.ws

# La Chaumière | French Market Cuisine

**L**OOKING for a classic French dining experience, complete with tablecloths and vested waiters? Longing to converse with your dining companions without shouting out your lungs? Desirous of fine service that appears when needed and disappears just as quickly? La Chaumière might be the answer.

Since 1978, La Chaumière has been one of Calgary's go-to restaurants for major events, corporate lunches (where every dish is under $20!) and romantic dinners. Over that time, little has changed (albeit they moved to a new space a number of years ago), proving that sometimes classics are keepers.

Executive chef/partner Bob Matthews, a talented local boy, creates a menu that draws from the wealth of French cuisine: veal sweetbreads on creamed spinach; saddle of lamb; braised escargots with mushrooms and bacon. But he infuses the list with Asian touches (he cooked at the Canadian embassy in Tokyo for a decade) in dishes such as grilled tuna with tempura vegetables and ponzu sauce; avocado in curry dressing; and baked sablefish in a green pea and wasabi crust. Frequent changes keep the menu—and the kitchen staff—from getting stale.

Service is under the watchful eye of co-owners Joe Mathes and Joseph D'Angelus, two professionals with a lifetime of experience. And great wine knowledge. They host one of the best wine cellars in the city: over 800 labels heavy in classic French and Italian reds. (There's a small cellar dining room, too.) They run a tight, well-honed ship. The dining experience at La Chaumière unfolds seamlessly and rolls smoothly through an evening.

So relax. Classics are worth the time.

**Address**
139 – 17 Avenue SW

**Phone**
403.228.5690

**Hours**
Monday – Friday
11:45 am – 2 pm

Monday – Saturday
5:30 pm – close

**Reservations**
Recommended

**Cards**
V, MC, AE

**Drinks**
Full bar
Call for corkage details

**Outdoor Dining**
Patio

**Noise**
◁ – ◁))

**Price Range**
$$ – $$$$

**Website**
lachaumiere.ca

# Laurier Lounge

French Boutique

SINCE 2005, Laurier Lounge has been Calgary's go-to place for fondue. The restaurant in the century-old Stanley House has served up buckets of cheese, broth and chocolate fondue and balanced it with an eclectic, French-influenced menu and a short, attractive, well-priced wine list.

But owner Martin Maheux (from Quebec City) has always had higher goals for his restaurant. So he recently partnered with chef Ryan O'Flynn (originally from Edmonton) to raise the bar to full French fluency. O'Flynn brings an impressive level of kitchen skill honed by a number of years in European kitchens.

An onion tarte Tatin ($11) at dinner showcases a marinated sous-vide onion baked under a pastry crust and served as a hot appetizer. The caramelization brings a sweetness to the onion so it almost resembles an apple. Divine. The chopped smoked salmon bruschetta ($9) is laced with mustard and capers in this gentle, cold appetizer. Terrific. And a cassoulet ($27), made with cannellini beans, duck confit and crisp pork belly, is made in a shallow dish to create extra crust—the best part.

The rest of the menu is packed with French classics such as beef bourguignon, bouillabaisse and duck à l'orange. The duck has a different spin though, done as it is over poutine. Laurier may be French, but they know how to throw in some fun quirks, too.

Laurier also looks the part of a small French bistro. Petite rooms create a cozy tone, and on summer days, the deck is a Calgary classic. And you can still get a great fondue.

**Address**
1111 – 7 Street SW

**Phone**
403.228.3771

**Hours**
Tuesday – Friday
8 am – 2:30 pm

Saturday & Sunday
9 am – 2 pm

Sunday – Thursday
3:30 pm – 10 pm

Friday & Saturday
3:30 pm – 11 pm

**Reservations**
Recommended
Not accepted Saturday &
Sunday, 9 am – 2 pm

**Cards**
V, MC, AE, Debit

**Drinks**
Full bar
Corkage $20/bottle

**Outdoor Dining**
Deck

**Noise**
◁) – ◁))

**Price Range**
$$ – $$$$

**Website**
laurierlounge.com

# Le Villa | Steak & Seafood

THE area west of Sarcee used to be a restaurant wasteland. Recently we've seen the arrival of good independents and a few reliable chains, but for years, there were only two places worth recommending: the Little Chef (now retired) and Le Villa.

Le Villa is in a strip mall and has a dining room and a lounge, plus a patio that's been glassed in. Heated by a central fireplace and a few furnace vents, the "patio" seems to be the destination of choice here. It's like eating outside but being fully inside, and it works even in very chilly weather.

The "patio" provides a great backdrop for the meaty cuisine of Rick Chuk, owner and chef. He's an experienced chef and grill cook, having worked the kitchen at Buchanan's for 16 years. His menu features various cuts of Certified Angus beef perfectly cooked and served with a variety of sauces (the port-Stilton is a personal favourite), but also includes things like rack of lamb, roast duck breast and bison short ribs. To balance the red meat, there are choices such as pan-fried steelhead with seared scallops, hollandaise and lobster risotto. Plus classics like coquilles St. Jacques and lobster bisque.

These are generous, classically prepared and presented plates, priced in the $20s and $30s at dinner and well served by a friendly staff. Lunch includes omelettes, salads, steak sandwiches, prime rib melts and such, more in the teens and low $20s.

As we were finishing this book, Chuk announced he would be opening a second Le Villa on 4th Street. I think Mission could use a good steakhouse.

**Address**
404, 1851 Sirocco Drive SW

**Phone**
403.217.9699

**Hours**
Tuesday – Friday
11:30 am – close

Saturday – Monday
5 pm – close

**Outdoor Dining**
Indoor "patio"

**Noise**
◁ – ◁))

---

**Address**
1800 – 4 Street SW

**Phone**
TBA

**Hours**
TBA

**Outdoor Dining**
Patio

**Noise**
TBA

---

**Common Info**

**Reservations**
Recommended

**Cards**
V, MC, AE, Debit

**Drinks**
Full bar
Corkage $20/bottle

**Price Range**
$$ – $$$$

**Website**
levilla.ca

# Leo Fu's

Chinese
(Szechuan & Mandarin)

WHEN Catherine is out for the evening and I'm left to eat on my own, I may whip up a nice omelette or some ratatouille. Or I may just call over to Leo Fu's and order chicken wings and some spicy seafood noodles. I know the food will be hot and tasty, the chicken wings—from some of the biggest chickens in the world—will be permeated with an oily Szechuan goodness, and the noodles will be packed with seafood. I also know that, in spite of my appetite, there'll be enough left over for lunch.

I've been frequenting Leo Fu's since the mid-1980s when John and Katy Koo ran the place with their family. The family is grown now and have their own kids and John is gone, but Leo Fu's lives on, still with the Koo family at the helm. In the early days, their combination of Mandarin and Szechuan food—General Tso's chicken, beef with black bean sauce, Szechuan dumplings, Szechuan string beans or eggplant—was a break from the proliferation of Peking-style places. And in all those years, no one has successfully replicated Leo Fu's formula.

Much of their success has to do with proprietary recipes passed down in the family, combined with a commitment to quality. The spice level and fried nature of some of the food may not be to everyone's taste, but there's no arguing about the quality. The salt and pepper seafood is light and crisp, and even their take on ginger beef is unique. And just once, try their Peking duck—gorgeous.

And don't forget the chicken wings.

**Address**
511 – 70 Avenue SW

**Phone**
403.255.2528

**Hours**
Monday – Friday
11:30 am – 2 pm

Sunday – Thursday
4:30 pm – 10 pm

Friday & Saturday
4:30 pm – 11 pm

**Reservations**
Recommended

**Cards**
V, MC, AE, Debit

**Drinks**
Full bar
Corkage $15/bottle

**Outdoor Dining**
None

**Noise**
🔊

**Price Range**
$$ – $$$

**Website**
No

# The Libertine

Modern Pub

**W**ITH 8,000 square feet spread over two floors, a lively patio and open windows that spill music onto Stephen Avenue, you might assume the Libertine is a pub. Once inside, the throb of music, the smiling and decidedly good-looking staff (both female and male), and the maze of bars and booths might enhance that notion.

And, you'd be correct.

But the Libertine is one of a new breed, that of "modern pub." So in addition to the 18 North American craft beers on tap and numerous wines by the glass, it also has remarkably good food. At first glance, the menu is deceiving—it looks like a simple list of sandwiches and flatbreads with a few obligatory pizzas and appetizers. Look deeper and you'll see sandwiches like a Moroccan-spiced lamb meat loaf one with red pepper sauce on a toasted baguette, and a clubhouse built with duck confit, bacon and smoked Gouda. These are not your typical pub sandwiches. Same goes for the pizzas. There's one with crimini, oyster and shiitake mushrooms combined with pesto and pine nuts. And another of house-made boar sausage with beer-braised onions and a Dijon gastrique. (In a pub? I'm not kidding.)

Not only are the ideas good, but the execution follows through. Nice crust on the pizzas, good sauces, well-distributed ingredients. Smart.

And if you'd like to bring the gang, the Libertine will do a whole pig roast with five days notice. These are huge feasts where you can pick your own slice of hog and all the cracklin' you want. Now that's what pub grub should be.

**Address**
233 Stephen Avenue SW

**Phone**
403.265.3665

**Hours**
Monday – Saturday
11 am – 2 am

**Reservations**
Accepted

**Cards**
V, MC, AE, Debit

**Drinks**
Full bar
No corkage

**Outdoor Dining**
Patio

**Noise**
 –

**Price Range**
$$

**Website**
thelibertine.ca

downtown
calgary

# Little New York

**Mediterranean**
**New Age**

**B**ACK in the 1930s during a local oil boom, the community of Longview popped up and acquired the nickname of Little New York. There was even a neighbouring Little Chicago (so nicknamed, though the official designation was Royalties), but when the oil boom went bust, so did it. Longview, luckily, lives on.

And so does its nickname, including in the name of this eatery. Little New York Bistro is a large, square 50-seat space built out of logs. Big wooden tables and chairs and an open ceiling add to the atmosphere, but delicate Moroccan runners top the tables, softening the look. It's owned by a Moroccan family who used to work at the Longview Steakhouse (which has an entry in this book) before opening their own place.

The lunch menu is mostly diner fare of sandwiches and burgers, but there are often Mediterranean specials such as couscous with roasted chicken, caramelized raisins and vegetables. We ordered a couple of soup and sandwich specials: the chicken club with soup and the chicken wrap with soup. Both were good, simple combinations of high-quality ingredients. The chicken in the club was freshly grilled and sliced, the bacon crisp, the tomatoes ripe, the bread an OK brand of whole wheat. The cauliflower-leek soup served with it was silky, lively and skilfully made.

In the evening, a Mediterranean bistro tone infuses braised lamb shanks with a Moroccan ras el hanout spice blend and piques seared mahi mahi with a cucumber-avocado aioli. There are escargots in a parsley sauce and mussels in a tarragon cream, too. That's some serious food, worthy of Little New York.

**Address**
108 Morrison Road
(Highway 22)
Longview

**Phone**
403.558.0000

**Hours**
Mother's Day – October:
Sunday – Thursday
10 am – 9 pm

Friday & Saturday
10 am – 10 pm

November – Mother's Day:
Call for hours

**Reservations**
Recommended,
especially for groups

**Cards**
V, MC, Debit

**Drinks**
Full bar
Corkage $15/bottle

**Outdoor Dining**
2 patios

**Noise**
🔊 – 🔊

**Price Range**
$ – $$

**Website**
No

# The Living Room

Contemporary
Interactive

**Address**
514 – 17 Avenue SW

**Phone**
403.228.9830

**Hours**
Daily
11:30 am – 2 pm
5 pm – close

**Reservations**
Recommended

**Cards**
V, MC, AE, Debit

**Drinks**
Full bar
Corkage $15/bottle

**Outdoor Dining**
Patio

**Noise**
◁) – ◁))

**Price Range**
$$ – $$$$

**Website**
livingroomrestaurant.ca

**A** GOOD patio is a thing of beauty. We Calgarians love to eat and drink outside whenever we can. (Anything above 10°C and sunny is fair game.) But some patios and decks are sketchy; you're so often breathing bus exhaust or deafened by Harleys. Not at the Living Room where tall elms shelter a walled and remarkably discreet patio. Heaters, fireplaces and a good windbreak keep this south-facing space serviceable longer than many.

The patio isn't the only reason to visit the Living Room. The food—head-scratchingly labelled Contemporary Interactive—is distinctly good. The "interactive" part includes things you eat by hand or can handle in some non-knife-and-fork way, like fondues, flatbreads, oysters, roast chicken and charcuterie. The "contemporary" part of the equation pairs roasted cauliflower, English peas and bacon with crisp veal sweetbreads and tops a stylized poutine of fried potatoes and apples with eight-year-aged cheddar and duck confit.

A simple chicken burger is constructed with chopped chicken rather than ground meat and is elevated by a bit of cranberry and a fine house-baked bun. The roasted cauliflower soup (they seem to have a thing for cauliflower here) is silky and sweet, a regal tribute to the normally bottom-bin vegetable.

The team that brought us the Living Room has recently opened Anejo, too, albeit with some new partners. The redo of the former 4 St. Rose has created a party-Mexican spot that hosts over 100 tequilas (and OK Mexican food). Good for a shot of the agave liquor after dinner at the Living Room, only a few blocks away.

# Longview Steakhouse

**Global Steakhouse**

Nestled in the Foothills south of Calgary, Longview is known for the great view, beef jerky, Ian Tyson and Longview Steakhouse. But this is a steakhouse with a difference.

Sure there are steaks: really fine steaks, perfectly cooked and served in a rustic farmhouse setting. But if French bistro fare is to your liking, you'll find seafood bisque, chausson d'escargot and roasted duck breast in a pear sauce. And if you'd like a taste of Morocco, perhaps the b'stilla pie will satisfy you.

Or take, for instance, a bowl of Moroccan carrot soup, a daily lunch special on a recent visit. Permeated with the spices of Morocco, the soup was creamy but not heavy, one of the best carrot soups of my life. On the meaty side, there was another daily special, a fresh-ground strip loin burger topped with aged cheddar, roasted peppers, sautéed onions and prosciutto. Each element was perfect—flavours intense throughout, cooked to order just under medium, the whole thing, three-napkin juicy.

And the service? Exemplary. Some of the finest, and warmest, you'll find in this book. That's because Longview Steakhouse is run by Driss Belmoufid, a lifelong restaurant and hotel professional, and his family. They've lived in Longview since 1994 and know the community well. Their particular blend of Moroccan-French-Western cuisine and hospitality works perfectly in the ranching village.

Note: By the summer of 2014, they'll be moving to a new location on a hill overlooking Longview (where a long-gone community nicknamed Little Chicago was once perched). The new building will include eight hotel rooms, too.

**Address**
102 Morrison Road
(Highway 22)
Longview

**Phone**
403.558.2000

**Hours**
Tuesday – Sunday
11:30 am – 2 pm
5 pm – 9:30 pm

**Reservations**
Recommended

**Cards**
V, MC, Debit

**Drinks**
Full bar
Corkage $11/bottle

**Outdoor Dining**
None

**Noise**
◁ – ◁)

**Price Range**
$$ – $$$

**Website**
No

# Mango Shiva

**W**HEN Penny Lane was demolished in 2007, some of the many restaurants there disappeared forever. But others moved and now thrive in new locations. Mango Shiva is one of those.

They took an old Dairy Queen—originally a taxidermy and gun shop in the MacKay and Dippie block (1909)—and converted it into perhaps the prettiest Indian restaurant in the city. It's a long, narrow brick and sandstone building that's been visually enlarged by placing mirrors behind latticed walls and bringing in transparent plastic chairs. The light from numerous lamps bounces off another mirrored wall studded with sculpted hands holding candles, and multi-coloured ornaments decorate the space. A small patio extends onto Stephen Avenue, and at the back of the room, a long communal table fronts an open kitchen.

The menu follows the forward-thinking style of the room. Butter chicken and mango chutney are folded into nans to create hand-held "nacos" ($13.75). Lamb chops are crusted with pistachios to create lambsicles ($17.75). Garam masala-seasoned lamb shanks are served with apricots, cherry-tomato tabbouleh and rogan josh ($27). There's even pork shoulder braised in a vindaloo curry ($23). When was the last time you saw pork on an Indian menu?

If you'd like even more creativity, go to Mango Shiva for weekend brunch where you'll find butter chicken and waffles ($15); vegetarian eggs Benedict with fenugreek hollandaise ($12); cardamom and raisin biscuits ($5); and poached eggs with lamb kofta ($15). And for something quick and simple, check out the weekday lunch buffet.

Seems Mango Shiva has all the angles covered.

**Address**
218 Stephen Avenue SW

**Phone**
403.290.1644

**Hours**
Monday – Thursday
11 am – 11 pm

Friday
11 am – close

Saturday
11:30 am – close

Sunday
11:30 am – 10 pm

**Reservations**
Recommended

**Cards**
V, MC, AE, Debit

**Drinks**
Full bar
Corkage $15/bottle

**Outdoor Dining**
Patio

**Noise**
◁) – ◁))

**Price Range**
$$ – $$$

**Website**
mangoshiva.com

downtown calgary

# Marathon

Ethiopian

I HAVE a friend who has difficulty at Marathon. It isn't the food. She actually likes the wats (stews) of lentils, beef, lamb and such. She enjoys the kick of berbere (the chili-infused spice mix used in Ethiopian cooking) and the richness of niter kibbeh (the spiced butter). She even likes the injera, the dense, spongy, crepey Ethiopian bread used to scoop up everything.

But she has a hard time eating it all with her hands. In traditional Ethiopian cuisine, you rip off a piece of injera and use it to pick up the foods, many of which are cooked into thick wats. My friend, though, prefers cutlery. Which is fine—the staff will happily oblige.

As for me, I like eating with my hands. Whether it's hot dogs, sushi, fried chicken, doro alicha, lega tibs or yebeg wat, I love being up to my elbows in the good stuff. It just seems to taste better.

The Marathon has been a cutlery-optional eatery—and one of Calgary's favourite Ethiopian restaurants—since 1997. Their cuisine is popular with carnivores for its fine beef, chicken and lamb dishes, but is just as favoured by the vegetarian crowd for all the wonderful pulse and vegetable dishes. Owners Michael Bogala and Mimi Tewabach have built a loyal clientele from both camps. And everyone seems to like the traditional Ethiopian drink: coffee.

Now I just have to convince my friend to try eating all this good food with her hands.

**Address**
130 – 10 Street NW

**Phone**
403.283.6796

**Hours**
Monday – Saturday
11 am – 2 pm

Daily
5:30 pm – 10 pm

**Reservations**
Recommended

**Cards**
V, MC, Debit

**Drinks**
Beer & wine
Corkage $12/bottle

**Outdoor Dining**
None

**Noise**
◁ – ◁))

**Price Range**
$$ – $$$

**Website**
marathonethiopian.com

# Market | Farm to Table

**H**YPERLOCAL cuisine.

That's a term we're starting to hear more of. Sure, there's been an emphasis on local and seasonal foods for a few years, but now some chefs and restaurateurs are taking it to the next level by, say, setting up hives and producing their own honey or contracting a local farm to grow the restaurant's produce or making as many items as possible in-house. That's the direction Market is taking.

Opened in early 2013, Market is a long agro-urban room with an open kitchen at the back. In that kitchen you'll see a big white booth, similar to a pop cooler, filled with greenery. It's Market's Urban Cultivator, a contraption that grows their fresh herbs. Market also bakes their own bread, churns their own cheeses, cures their own meats and even makes their own soda pop. If there were room in the parking lot, I'm sure they'd set up a pasture for cows and pigs.

The result is fresh food creatively prepared. In-house kimchi and pickled shallots enhance a gentle tuna crudo. House-smoked bacon adds to the refined rusticity of a tasty kale Caesar salad. An herb emulsion born of the Urban Cultivator kicks a steak 'n' tater dish of juicy hanger steak, potato aligot (mashed potatoes mixed with cheese) and sautéed Hotchkiss chard up a notch. And house-churned yuzu ice cream layered into sandwiches constructed with homemade chocolate chip cookies finishes a meal with élan.

Market's food is backed up by a service staff that is confidently professional and personable. Combined with the food, it makes Market a prime destination for farm-to-table, hyperlocal cuisine.

**Address**
718 – 17 Avenue SW

**Phone**
403.474.4414

**Hours**
Sunday – Wednesday
11 am – 11 pm

Thursday – Saturday
11 am – 1 am

**Reservations**
Recommended

**Cards**
V, MC, AE, Debit

**Drinks**
Full bar
No corkage

**Outdoor Dining**
Patio

**Noise**
◁)) – ◁))

**Price Range**
$$ – $$$$

**Website**
marketcalgary.ca

# Mehtab | Indian

**R**UN by a family from Northern India, Mehtab features the tandoor-roasted dishes of their area, such as tandoori chicken or prawns, lamb seekh kebabs and lamb chops. They even do paneer tikka, house-made cheese that's marinated in ginger, garlic, lemon and other spices and then cooked in the tandoor—a great way to add flavour to the essentially blank palate of paneer.

They make interesting non-tandoor dishes, too, such as the chicken badami with its sauce of cashews, cherries and almonds. It's a thick, mild dish that offers a different turn on the typical butter chicken. For a second dish, try the handi chicken cooked in a cashew paste and seasoned with saffron. Then there's lamb rarajosh, which combines chunks of lamb with minced lamb in a thick black pepper sauce. Delightful. Most dishes are in the $13 to $16 range, reasonably priced for the quantity and quality.

A few other things about this food. First, it's very mild. That's their standard. So if you like it spicy, say so up front. Second, I was impressed with the overall quality and use of ingredients—the meats, especially. Large pieces and lots of them, very little gristle and bone. No hunting around in the sauce for them either. Third, they don't use ghee, the clarified butter most Indian places use. Instead, they cook with canola, and comparatively small amounts of it. So the food is not at all oily. And fourth, they use organic spices. Nice.

Just be sure to ask for more heat if that's the way you like it.

**Address**
2008, 120 – 5 Avenue W
Cochrane

**Phone**
403.851.0100

**Hours**
Sunday – Friday
11:30 am – 9 pm

Saturday
4 pm – 9 pm

**Reservations**
Accepted

**Cards**
V, MC, AE, Debit

**Drinks**
Full bar
Corkage $10/bottle

**Outdoor Dining**
None

**Noise**
◁)

**Price Range**
$$

**Website**
mehtabrestaurant.com

# Mercato

WHEN Mercato opened on 4th Street SW, it was mostly a market with a small coffee bar. The demand for food quickly outstripped the capacity, so the dining area was enlarged and enlarged and then enlarged again. Now it's a small market with a restaurant that seats nearly 100 people. The only way to answer the still-increasing demand was to open a second location.

So they did.

The Mercato in West Springs, which opened in 2012, is split into a full-scale Italian market and a full-scale restaurant, physically divided by a large, long, open kitchen. High seats wrap around the kitchen bar in a creative zigzag fashion, and lower seats and tables are spread around the spacious dining room. The latest Mercato gives you much more elbow room for chowing down on the lamb sirloin with tomato-walnut pesto or the hand-rolled gnocchi with mascarpone, sage and pistachios.

We like sitting at the new zigzag bar. It's great for two if you can nab a corner so that you're facing each other. And it works almost as well for four. Perched there, you can watch the heavy lifting done by the cooks just a metre or so away. And inhale the fresh wafts of hearty Italian cooking.

Mercato (both locations serve basically the same menu) is certainly one of the pricier Italian places around. But the portions are large and suitable for sharing. So you don't need to order as many dishes as you might think. We find that a salad, an appetizer and a pasta—even the smaller of the two pasta sizes offered—is fine for the both of us.

**Address**
2224 – 4 Street SW

**Phone**
403.263.5535

**Hours**
Daily
11:30 am – 2 pm
5:30 pm – close

**Drinks**
Full bar
No corkage

**Outdoor Dining**
Patio

---

**Address**
5000, 837 – 85 Street SW

**Phone**
403.263.6996

**Hours**
Tuesday – Sunday
11:30 am – 2 pm
5 pm – close

**Drinks**
Beer, wine, grappa
No corkage

**Outdoor Dining**
None

---

**Common Info**

**Reservations**
Highly recommended

**Cards**
V, MC, AE, Debit

**Noise**
◁) – ◁))

**Price Range**
$$$ – $$$$

**Website**
mercatogourmet.com

# Mimo

**M**IMO is the eternal restaurant. As long as Isabel Da Costa and her family keep grilling huge shrimp and curing their own chorizo, Mimo will continue to prosper. That's in spite of its wonky location in the back row of a strip mall called Little Saigon. Those who never venture east of Deerfoot are missing some fine Portuguese food.

For almost 30 years, Mimo has served the best pork and clams and the finest Portuguese barbecued chicken in town. The fact that they are the only Portuguese restaurant for miles around should not lessen this accolade. Da Costa is a master of the cuisine, having grown up in the Azores islands and later learning the recipes from her mother.

She douses most things liberally with piri-piri sauce, a dense mash of chilies, garlic and spices in rich Portuguese olive oil. It perks up the barbecued chicken, adds a zing to the pork loin and takes shellfish to a whole new level.

Also of particular note is Da Costa's presunto and chorizo. Cured in-house by husband John, the presunto—Portugal's answer to serrano and prosciutto hams—is salty and not overly greasy, on par with the aforementioned hams. The chorizo is smoky heaven, meaty with just the right amount of fat. And unlike New World chorizos, it's not terribly spicy.

Service is often handled by Da Costa herself and her two daughters. They make a wonderful team, always professional and always ready to laugh. It keeps Da Costa and her restaurant young. And eternal.

**Address**
203, 4909 – 17 Avenue SE
(Little Saigon Centre)

**Phone**
403.235.3377

**Hours**
Monday – Thursday
11 am – 10 pm

Friday & Saturday
11 am – 11 pm

**Reservations**
Recommended

**Cards**
V, MC, Debit

**Drinks**
Full bar
Corkage $20.95/bottle

**Outdoor Dining**
None

**Noise**
◁))

**Price Range**
$$ – $$$

**Website**
No

# Model Milk | Contemporary Bistro

**C**HEF/PARTNER Justin Leboe and the Concorde Group did a very smart thing when opening the appropriately named Model Milk. They took the loading dock of a former dairy (the Model Milk Company) and converted the high-ceilinged space into a restaurant.

The multi-level loading dock provided the partners with a see-and-be-seen dining theatre where the open kitchen takes prominence on the middle of the three levels. The kitchen is a culinary showcase surrounded by a few tall seats for the most inquisitive diners and from which heavenly aromas emerge.

The main, lower-level dining area is surrounded by brick—essentially no wood was used in the 1935-construction of the art deco dairy—and tends to get quite noisy. One great feature is a long, central line of tabletops that can be pushed together along a heavy metal beam to form a single table for large groups. It can also be spread apart for couples or small groups. Simple, but effective.

Leboe's food jumps with creativity. He prepares P.E.I. halibut with crisp Italian guanciale (cured pork jowl) and sauerkraut emulsion. Oh my. His fricassee of calamari, prepared with more guanciale, Japanese edamame and Spanish pimentón is another cross-cultural effort that redefines calamari dishes. Loaded with rich flavours, it looks like a plate of pasta.

Leboe plays with texture as much as flavour in dishes such as his Dungeness crab salad with crunchy macadamia nuts and his shrimp and grits with a fried egg. Wonderful! And try The Burger, topped with a mushroom ragout and cheese curds. One of the best burgers anywhere.

**Address**
308 – 17 Avenue SW

**Phone**
403.265.7343

**Hours**
Sunday – Wednesday
5 pm – 11 pm

Thursday – Saturday
5 pm – 2 am

**Reservations**
Recommended

**Cards**
V, MC, AE, Debit

**Drinks**
Full bar
Corkage $25/bottle

**Outdoor Dining**
Small patio

**Noise**
◁)) – ◁))

**Price Range**
$$$ – $$$$

**Website**
modelmilk.ca

# Moti Mahal

Indian (Kashmiri)

Tucked into the backside of a building off 14th Street south of 17th Avenue SW, Moti Mahal doesn't at first look like one of Calgary's most prominent Indian restaurants. Its hidden location seems like it shouldn't work, but with well over two decades of service in the Calgary scene, Moti has a multitude of fans willing to seek it out.

Moti's cuisine is Kashmiri, the creamier, nuttier, fruitier side of Indian food. The dishes here sound familiar (most Indian dishes use the same names, though ingredients and preparation techniques may vary across the country), but they are often more full-bodied in Kashmir than elsewhere in India. The korma at Moti, for instance, available with chicken, lamb or prawns, is laced with almonds, raisins, cardamom and more cream than you'd find in a Punjabi version. So rich, so good. The papaya prawn curry is filled with cream, papaya and saffron. This is intense Indian food, intense as much for its richness as its spiciness.

Moti's space is the perfect backdrop for the food, decorated as it is in colourful trappings. An L-shaped room, it's long and narrow with two rows of tables filling the space.

At lunchtime, an L-shaped buffet echoes the room and is quickly pillaged by hordes looking for a good feed. I like that they bake the nan fresh so it's delivered to you hot and soft instead of cooling on the buffet. And they don't dumb down the buffet—each dish retains its own flavour integrity and is prepared as skilfully as at dinner.

It's that kind of consistency that keeps Moti among the best.

**Address**
1805 – 14 Street SW

**Phone**
403.228.9990

**Hours**
Monday – Friday
11:30 am – 1:30 pm

Sunday – Thursday
5:30 pm – 9:30 pm

Friday & Saturday
5:30 pm – 10:30 pm

**Reservations**
Accepted

**Cards**
V, MC, AE, Debit

**Drinks**
Full bar
Corkage $15/bottle

**Outdoor Dining**
None

**Noise**
◁ – ◁))

**Price Range**
$$ – $$$

**Website**
motimahal.ca

# Muse

New Canadian

**W**ITH new ownership comes change. So when Stephen Deere and Heather Wighton, two young but seasoned industry professionals, took over Muse in late 2012, they brought in chef JP Pedhirney to help conceive a contemporary menu of dishes like pork confit with asparagus, lentil ragout and apple mostarda, and a Dungeness crab salad with macadamia nuts, apples and avocado mousse. It's food that focuses on local ingredients (when possible), classic technique and multiple ingredients on the plate. Each mouthful reveals a nuance of flavour or a change of texture.

The new owners haven't done a lot to the look of the place; that will come in time. The multi-level restaurant maintains a Mardi Gras meets Cirque du Soleil tone in its collection of small dining areas. (It always feels to me that there should be a stage somewhere featuring contortionists or jugglers.) For now, Muse maintains its comfortable, familiar tones.

A beef tartare with toasted Sidewalk Citizen bread provides a combination of silky smooth beef, crunchy toast, tart cornichons and creamy egg yolk, an experience as much about texture as taste. Lovely. And the crab salad sings of the sea, landed with nuts and avocado. This is food that's best savoured slowly to catch the subtlety of it.

Don't miss the wine list at Muse. Like the food, it is well conceived, deep in variety, long in quality. From good tastes by the glass (for reasonable prices) to top-drawer, exclusive wines, it serves to make the Muse experience a fine one.

**Address**
107–10A Street NW

**Phone**
403.670.6873

**Hours**
Tuesday – Sunday
5 pm – close

**Reservations**
Recommended

**Cards**
V, MC, AE, Debit

**Drinks**
Full bar
Corkage $25/bottle

**Outdoor Dining**
Small balcony

**Noise**
◁ – ◁))

**Price Range**
$$$ – $$$$

**Website**
muserestaurant.ca

# Namskar Indian (Northern)

**T**HE fact that Namskar was originally built to be an Italian restaurant should not in the least deter you from now trying it for some of the best Northern Indian food in the city. The look—with two high-ceilinged rooms divided by an entry foyer—is neutral enough to accommodate the flavours of either the Indian subcontinent or the Italian boot. Besides, the Indian food is tasty enough to forget the Italian origins.

Namskar owner Trilochan Sekhon puts great care and attention into his food. A simple curry jumps with the flavour of freshly roasted and blended herbs and spices, a dal makhani of lentils and kidney beans is decadently rich and addictive, and a lamb rogan josh packs your mouth with exotic flavours. I find myself lingering on one dish while ignoring the others. Then I force myself to move on and get stuck on the next dish. Before I know it, I'm stuffed. (And I always order enough for leftovers.)

Regardless of all of Namskar's fine dishes, I have two weaknesses here: the seafood and the breads. The prawn masala is a parade of flavours, and the butter prawns take the whole concept of butter *anything* up a whole bunch of notches. (And you'll never look at butter chicken the same again.) Add in any of the nans and I'm happy. (Although I'm basically a plain nan guy, the cashew-coconut-pistachio-raisin Peshawari nan is great and almost a meal in itself.)

When it comes down to it, I've never been disappointed by a single dish at Namskar, regardless of the duality of the setting.

**Address**
202 – 16 Avenue NE

**Phone**
403.230.4447

**Hours**
Monday – Friday
11:30 am – 2 pm

Monday – Thursday
5 pm – 10 pm

Friday – Sunday
4:30 pm – 10 pm

**Reservations**
Recommended

**Cards**
V, MC, AE, Debit

**Drinks**
Full bar
Corkage $10/bottle

**Outdoor Dining**
None

**Noise**
🔊

**Price Range**
$ – $$$

**Website**
namskar.com

# National Beer Hall

North American
Comfort Food

IREMEMBER when beer halls came with pickled eggs, terry cloth-topped tables, a jukebox, sawdust-covered floors, the smell of stale beer, cranky male (as in, no women) waiters in white shirts with arm bands and two-and-a-juice (that's two glasses of draft and one of tomato juice) for 50 cents. And when those halls had no windows or patios. (It's really not that long ago.)

Wow, how things have changed. The National Beer Hall on 17th Avenue has floor-to-ceiling wraparound windows that open onto a sidewalk patio. Inside, a bank of TV screens outlines the 72 North American craft beers they have on tap, plus the additional 32 in bottles. The National on 10th—with 560 seats—has an eight-lane bowling alley! (And look for a third National in West Hills soon.)

Cheerful male and female staff in star-logoed black T-shirts deliver pints and burgers to customers seated at long wooden tables inside (28 folks per table!) or under shady umbrellas outside. The Nationals are built for groups, for socializing and for liveliness. They're loud.

The smell of rotisserie chicken, duck confit and roasted porchetta fills both spots, and a pint of draft (a full 20 ounces) sells for $8.50. (You can pay over $40 a bottle for some specialty brews that roll up to 15% alcohol.) The menu features burgers cooked to order from house-ground Spring Creek beef. (Want a medium-rare burger? This is the place.) There are pork pies and Cobb salads, prime rib dinners and poutines, and yes, somewhere on the National's menu there are pickled eggs, scooped from a one-gallon glass jar of pickling brine. Some things never change.

**Address**
550 – 17 Avenue SW

**Phone**
403.229.0226

**Outdoor Dining**
Patio

**Noise**
◁)) – ◁))

---

**Address**
341 – 10 Avenue SW

**Phone**
403.770.2323

**Outdoor Dining**
Rooftop Patio

**Noise**
◁))

 downtown calgary

---

**Common Info**

**Hours**
Daily
11 am – late

**Reservations**
Accepted

**Cards**
V, MC, AE, Debit

**Drinks**
Full bar
No corkage

**Price Range**
$ – $$$

**Website**
ntnl.ca

# Nirvana

Indian

IF you're looking for a good meal in the Falconridge-Castleridge area of northeast Calgary, there is a multitude of choices, many of which are either Indian or Pakistani. One of the places that keeps drawing me back is Nirvana, a large and lovely restaurant that serves food from across India.

Nirvana is filled with Indian marble, carved wood and fountains (occasionally with flowing water), all under a domed ceiling. The two-level dining room is sided by a sweet shop (it's all owned by the Bombay Sweet Shop folks) and sits above a large basement banquet hall. In total, seating exceeds 400.

The menu includes dishes from Mumbai, Delhi, Hyderabad, Goa and the Punjab, spanning a broad expanse of the country. But one thing you won't find on the menu is beef. (You won't find pork either, but you likely expected that.) Many customers in this area are observant Hindus, so beef stays on the sidelines.

In its place, you'll find chicken, seafood, lamb and goat. (And it's great goat. Goat is so often just bone and gristle; here, it's meaty and fall-off-the-bone tender.) Oddly, given that butter chicken is a relatively new dish and this is such a traditional place, they have one of the best butter chickens in the city. There are loads of vegetarian dishes here, too. The dals are rich and flavourful but not excessively hot, and the paneers are dense and well paired with vegetables.

For the best variety, check out the lunchtime buffet ($15), which is filled with flavour end to end. Often there are no labels, but that just adds to the fun.

**Address**
1009, 5075 Falconridge Boulevard NE

**Phone**
403.590.9797

**Hours**
Daily
11 am – 11 pm

**Reservations**
Accepted

**Cards**
V, MC, AE, Debit

**Drinks**
Full bar
No corkage

**Outdoor Dining**
None

**Noise**
◁ – ◁»

**Price Range**
$$

**Website**
nirvanacalgary.com

# Notable

## Gourmet Comfort

WHEN Michael Noble was building Notable, many people shook their heads. "In Montgomery?" they queried. "Away from the action?" they continued. "Won't work," they declared.

But the head shakers somehow missed the huge mass of hungry and under-restauranted inhabitants of the great northwest. They forgot about the proximity of Foothills Hospital and the University of Calgary. And they ignored the abundant free parking in the neighbourhood.

Noble knew what he was doing. This is a chef who has represented Canada (twice!) at the Bocuse d'Or, also known as the world championship of chefs. He was the first Canadian to appear on TV's *Iron Chef*—the original Japanese version. He has countless medals from international competitions hanging on the walls at Notable, and many local chefs credit much of their knowledge to time spent with him. When *Avenue*, Calgary's major city magazine, created a controversial cover featuring a bunch of local chefs in *Last Supper* poses, guess who was asked to play Jesus? Yeah, he knows what he's doing.

Notable purports to be about great food, not fine dining. And the tasty, casual plates back this up. The soup and the burger change frequently, but if mushroom soup is available when you visit, check it out. Fabulously creamy and mushroomy. Anything off the big rotisserie—roast chicken, lamb leg, rack of pork, prime rib—is wonderful. As are the seared East Coast scallops with bacon dressing. But leave room for Noble's signature Stilton cheesecake with rhubarb compote.

And don't worry about the odd location. It works. Plus look for a second Notable to open in Inglewood, likely in 2014.

**Address**
4611 Bowness Road NW

**Phone**
403.288.4372

**Hours**
Tuesday – Thursday
11:30 am – 10 pm

Friday
11:30 am – 11 pm

Saturday
11 am – 11 pm

Sunday
11 am – 9 pm

**Reservations**
Recommended

**Cards**
V, MC, AE, Debit

**Drinks**
Full bar
Corkage $25/bottle

**Outdoor Dining**
Patio

**Noise**
◁)) – ◁))

**Price Range**
$$ – $$$

**Website**
notabletherestaurant.ca

# O Bistro

**O**KAY, the name: it's *O* the letter, not *o* the number. The *O* stands for Olivier, as in owner Olivier Gouin. Schooled by his father Jean-François (a consummate saucier and owner of Canmore's Chez François) in the intricacies of classic French cuisine and also trained at SAIT, Gouin has opened his own place.

The tiny 26-seat room, the original Crazyweed location, is packed with an eclectic energy. An additional 17-seat, streetside patio brightens the restaurant in nice weather. (In cold weather, try not to sit too close to the door or you'll be hit by a chilly blast every time it opens.)

There's an eclectic range to O's menu. You'll find items like escargots gratinée, bouillabaisse and cassoulet from the traditional school; Brome Lake duck poutine and a lamb burger from the contemporary movement; and duck wontons and butter chicken from the international scene. It's a style that fits the eclectic tone of Canmore well.

My "chien chaud" here was memorable with its grilled Mennonite andouille sausage topped with sautéed onions and peppers all slid into a soft sesame-seeded bun. A roasted red pepper soup served with the dog was rich, creamy, beautifully seasoned and abundant—a serious bowl of soup. My whole meal jumped with flavour and character.

O Bistro has the support of a tight, professional team, right from the cooks to the black-clad servers. Many speak fluent French, adding a little bonus to visitors from Quebec and France. And a touch more *eau* to the O Bistro mix.

**Address**
626 Main Street
Canmore

**Phone**
403.678.3313

**Hours**
Monday – Thursday
11 am – 10 pm

Friday – Sunday
9 am – 10 pm

**Reservations**
Accepted

**Cards**
V, MC, AE, Debit

**Drinks**
Full bar
Corkage $15/bottle

**Outdoor Dining**
Patio

**Noise**
◁ – ◁))

**Price Range**
$$ – $$$$

**Website**
restaurantobistro.com

# Open Range

**T**HIS page is for carnivores—unabashed, unapologetic meat eaters who consider bison enchiladas or chili-rubbed ribs to be good dinner starters. For those who can't decide between a venison meat loaf with salsa roja or a lamb shank braised with chorizo, ale, thyme and grainy Dijon. For those who think adding a side of yam fries with smoked-paprika mayo or some scalloped potatoes layered with Sylvan Star Gouda are fine vegetable choices to balance a meal.

That's because this page is for Open Range, one of the finest places to take your favourite meat fan and a definite must for out-of-towners who crave a hit of Alberta beef. Or some duck (seared breast with Riesling-braised apples and cider glaze). Or elk ("Diane" with organic cream, cipollini onions and redcurrant demi-glace). Or chicken (free-range with cranberry-chipotle glaze). Or wild boar (with wild mushroom-stuffed pork belly).

About that beef. Try the blackened New York; a demerara-crusted rib chop; the tenderloin on a pearl onion-chanterelle ragout; or the big old porterhouse. Expect a stellar experience. (A learned band of carnivores on *Breakfast Television* named Open Range Calgary's top steakhouse in 2013.)

You and your dining partners will likely enjoy the low-key, haute-ranch setting, too, right down to the barnboard and toasty fireplace. Plus the service.

For veggie munchers, there are three salads, plus a few seafood options for nautical types. Or seats at Open Range's attached seafood restaurant, Big Fish. (It's mighty tasty too.)

But this page is for the carnivores, those who are licking this page right now.

**Address**
1114 Edmonton Trail NE

**Phone**
403.277.3408

**Hours**
Daily
5 pm – close

**Reservations**
Recommended

**Cards**
V, MC, AE, Debit

**Drinks**
Full bar
Corkage $20/bottle
Free corkage Wednesdays

**Outdoor Dining**
None

**Noise**
◁)

**Price Range**
$$$

**Website**
open-range.ca

# Ox and Angela

Spanish Tapas

**B**EEN to Una Pizza + Wine? Did you wait in a long line? The 17th Avenue pizzeria doesn't take reservations, so the lineup can take awhile. When the owners saw this was a daily occurrence, they decided to open a second location, one that would take reservations so they could send some of their lineup there.

They found a spot a short distance east of Una, did some renos and opened Ox and Angela. They thought the name was unique enough not to be confused with any other one. And they were right. It works.

But they didn't try to replicate Una. Instead, they opted for a Spanish-influenced, mostly tapas-style restaurant with a separate lounge. The restaurant side is bright and white, with Spanish knick-knacks throughout and an open kitchen filling one end. The lounge side is darker, softer and livelier, a fine place for a cocktail or some tapas.

O & A's tapas menu is a true tapas menu: there's tortilla de España of potatoes and eggs; salt cod fritters; Serrano ham; and prawns with Espelette peppers. Prices range from $2.50 (gazpacho with fried bread) to $19 (scallops with more gazpacho and sesame). They do a couple of large items, too: a daily paella for two or three people at $28 and a 12-ounce Wagyu rib-eye at $36 (it's mighty tasty). On the beverage side, O & A has one of the better cocktail lists in the city—creative and, again, Spanish influenced.

Funny thing is, now Ox and Angela is usually full, and the lineup at Una is just as long as ever. Nice problem to have.

**Address**
528 – 17 Avenue SW

**Phone**
403.457.1432

**Hours**
Sunday – Thursday
11:30 am – 11 pm

Friday & Saturday
11:30 am – midnight

**Reservations**
Accepted

**Cards**
V, MC, AE, Debit

**Drinks**
Full bar
No corkage

**Outdoor Dining**
Patio

**Noise**
◁)) – ◁))

**Price Range**
$$ – $$$

**Website**
oxandangela.com

# Pfanntastic Pannenkoek

Dutch Pancakes

**W**AY back in my first restaurant guide, there's an entry about a meal we had with our 14-month-old niece, her first dinner in public. It was, quite predictably, a messy affair.

Fast forward to 2013 and young Meghan—with husband John—now has two kids of her own. Maddock, at four, has been in and out of restaurants since the day he was born; Wyatt, second-in-command at four months, is close behind. So we thought it was time to revisit our earlier experience, this time at one of our favourite family-friendly places: Pfanntastic Pannenkoek Haus (PPH).

Since 1997, PPH has been spinning Dutch pancakes—or pannenkoeken—in a small strip mall near the intersection of Glenmore and Crowchild. Their pancakes are thinner than the Stampede kind, closer to a crepe, but with all sorts of goodies cooked into them. There are two basic varieties: savoury, with the likes of bacon, mushrooms and cheese; and sweet, with apple and cinnamon and such. A single pancake is usually enough for a meal; most run $10 to $12, so they don't break the bank.

Maddock and I both ordered the same version: the potato-onion-bacon-cheese pancake. Both of us enjoyed the tasty flavours, although Maddock might have been a bit more interested in the cookies that came with his Dad's coffee. Wyatt seemed pretty unconcerned by any of the proceedings.

Through it all, the PPH staff handled our requests for coffee and cookies and pancake changes with aplomb. It was as seamless as a brunch with a four-year-old and an infant can be. And Meghan's table manners have much improved.

**Address**
2439 – 54 Avenue SW

**Phone**
403.243.7757

**Hours**
Wednesday – Friday
9 am – 8 pm

Saturday
8 am – 8 pm

Sunday
8 am – 3 pm

**Reservations**
Accepted all day
Wednesday – Friday
& Saturday after 4 pm

**Cards**
V, MC, AE, Debit

**Drinks**
Full bar
No corkage

**Outdoor Dining**
None

**Noise**
◁ – ◁))

**Price Range**
$ – $$

**Website**
dutchpancakes.ca

# Post Hotel

Local, Fresh Market

**I**'M waiting to order my club sandwich in the Post Hotel's loggy, lodgy dining room and listening to a couple across the room order their lunch.

"I want the eggs scrambled, not in an omelette," says the man in the yacht club sweatshirt. "And the salmon has to be lox, not smoked," he continues with a certain directorial arrogance. "No rolls. Toast. I want brown, not multi-grain. And not buttered. The orange juice *has* to be fresh-squeezed."

I wouldn't blame anyone within earshot for feeling a brief impulse to throttle him, but his server graciously accepts the order and moves on.

Moments later, my club sandwich arrives, perfectly presented, sided with double-dipped, ultra-crispy fries so hot I have to wait to pick them up. It's a great sandwich: the chicken breast warm and moist, the bacon warm and crisp, layers of avocado and ripe tomato. It's a classic. My server, the same one mentioned above, smiles an amiable smile.

That's the Post, professional to the core, service at the centre of an all-round excellent dining experience that wows guests, whether it's a casual breakfast or an elegant, top-end dinner. It's no wonder they keep knocking down major global hotel awards, including some from the *Wine Spectator* for one of the best wine lists in Canada (2,200 labels, 25,000 bottles!).

I've had many fine meals at the Post, some during the busy summer tourist and convention season, some during less busy months. And the quality never wavers. Even if the occasional customer is a pain. But they'd never say that. I dare say, they wouldn't even think it.

**Address**
200 Pipestone Road
Lake Louise

**Phone**
403.522.3989

**Hours**
Daily
7 am – 11 pm
11:30 am – 2 pm
5 pm – 10 pm

(Hotel closed
mid-October –
late November)

**Reservations**
Recommended

**Cards**
V, MC, AE, Debit

**Drinks**
Full bar
No corkage

**Outdoor Dining**
Small patio for dinner only

**Noise**
🔊

**Price Range**
$$ – $$$$

**Website**
posthotel.com

# Pulcinella

**P**ULCINELLA used to be a no-brainer. We'd slide into a table in the bright, white dining room and watch the cooks form Neapolitan pizzas and slide them into the huge oven, retrieving them only a minute or two later, hot and crispy. I'd order a Diavola pizza topped with spicy salami, Parmesan and mozzarella, Catherine would have a pizza margherita or a prosciutto and arugula one, and we'd be set (though sometimes the backside of the pies have been toastier than Catherine likes).

But then owner Domenic Tudda had to go and add a menu of appetizers and pastas—handmade gnocchi with fresh tomato sauce, gluten-free polenta lasagna, calamari in a lemony tomato sauce. Such choices!

And we've indulged in many. The pork and beef meatballs are superb. The spaghetti carbonara, made with pancetta and egg yolk, is divine. And the battered oyster mushrooms in Gorgonzola cream is one of the top mushroom dishes I've had anywhere, anytime. Delicate? Not in the least. Tasty? Oh, yeah.

The reason for the menu addition is simple. For a while, Tudda used an upstairs room as a separate restaurant for serving pastas and appetizers—but not pizzas. With his pizzas so popular, though, downstairs was always packed, while upstairs was not. So he brought the upstairs menu downstairs and started serving pizzas upstairs, too. Now people order a mix of dishes or, sometimes, no pizza at all.

It all works out. The pizza oven is as busy as ever, and the room continues to hop with energy. A visit just requires a bit more brain power these days.

**Address**
1147 Kensington Crescent NW

**Phone**
403.283.7793

**Hours**
Monday – Thursday
11:30 am – 11 pm

Friday & Saturday
11:30 am – midnight

Sunday
11:30 am – 10 pm

**Reservations**
Accepted

**Cards**
V, MC, AE, Debit

**Drinks**
Full bar
No corkage

**Outdoor Dining**
Deck off 2nd floor

**Noise**
◁)) – ◁))

**Price Range**
$$ – $$$

**Website**
pulcinella.ca

# Q

**Q** is the only restaurant in this book to fly the banner of Haute Cuisine. While the bulk of the dining world has become more and more casual over the past few years, Q has stayed staunchly "haute." It's the kind of place where dinner can be a customized chef's tasting menu of between three and eight courses (you choose the number) or it can be simply à la carte.

Chef/partner Michele Aurigemma is one of the most skilled and talented chefs in Calgary (he trained and worked with Marco Pierre White in London). His style is heavily influenced by his Italian-Mediterranean background as well as his Continental training, and he is constantly evolving as a chef. Haute Cuisine at Q should not be interpreted as stodgy and dull. This is still forward-looking food.

Take, for example, a chestnut soup with foie gras, puffed wheat and pine nuts. A creative start to dinner, wouldn't you say? Or consider his Parmesan custard with sopressata sausage, Brussels sprouts-truffle slaw and semolina crackers. Interesting. His dinner list goes on with pork belly served with compressed apple and tonka-bean gelée; borscht gnocchi with a smoked salmon roulade; and sous-vide duck breast with an almond and dehydrated mushroom salad. Nothing boring about this approach. Even the lunch menu is tantalizing, yet structured to get you in and out in the time desired.

It's all expertly served by partner Marcello Belvedere's experienced staff in Q's warren of dining rooms. And a Q bonus: the best view of the Peace Bridge, bar none.

## Haute Cuisine

**Address**
100 La Caille Place SW

**Phone**
403.262.5554

**Hours**
Monday – Friday
11:30 am – 1:30 pm

Monday – Saturday
5:30 pm – close

**Reservations**
Recommended

**Cards**
V, MC, AE, Debit

**Drinks**
Full bar
Corkage $25/bottle

**Outdoor Dining**
None

**Noise**
◁))

**Price Range**
$ – $$$$

**Website**
qhautecuisine.com

downtown calgary

# Ratatouille

**B**ACK in the 1990s, Bistro JoJo was one of the hottest spots around Calgary. Chef/restaurateur Mohammed Guelli served simple, classic French food there, and it was always enjoyable. But an offer to return to his native Morocco to run the food services at a plush beach resort took him away from Calgary.

Meanwhile daughter Nabila, who had grown up mostly in Calgary, received her chef certification from SAIT and travelled the world enhancing her skills. After a few years, she decided her own restaurant would be located here, in Britannia Plaza, near where many of JoJo's former customers live.

So in the spring of 2013, the younger Guelli opened Ratatouille, a 60-seat bistro that features a steel-topped bar, red velour-covered banquettes, and framed black and white photos of French scenes. The floor, an epoxy-coated, pebbled aggregate, adds an indoor-outdoor tone akin to the sidewalk cafés of France.

The scent of duck breast sautéed in Calvados ($32) and fillet mignon ($35) flamed with Armagnac rolls out of the kitchen, filling the room with lushness. The menu is filled with classics from entrecôte à la Bordelaise ($29) and bouillabaisse ($33) to frog legs marinière ($14) and cassoulet ($29). Preparations follow the classic mould and a seafood tajine adds a Moroccan touch. *Plats du jour* bring in daily alternatives.

Ratatouille has a calm, relaxed, neighbourhood tone (read: not noisy), the kind of place that's nice to walk to for a bowl of soup or a simple *plat du jour*. As the young Guelli says, "This is where I want to be. This is my home."

**Address**
829 – 49 Avenue SW
(Britannia Plaza)

**Phone**
403.719.1942

**Hours**
Monday – Friday
11 am – 2 pm

Monday – Saturday
5 pm – 10 pm

**Reservations**
Accepted

**Cards**
V, MC, AE, Debit

**Drinks**
Full bar
Corkage $25/bottle

**Outdoor Dining**
Patio in 2014

**Noise**
🔊

**Price Range**
$$$ – $$$$

**Website**
No

# Raw Bar

**Asian Fusion**

Sitting by the pool at Hotel Arts, enjoying the food and cocktails of Raw Bar, is one of Calgary's great summer treats. The Asian fusion cuisine is always bright, lively and light—perfect pool fare. And the cocktails, among the most creative in town, are nearly enough to tempt us away from our favoured wines.

I like sitting by the pool, too, because I've never been sold on the dark, loungy decor of Raw Bar itself. But that was slated to change in late summer, 2013, so by the time you read this, it should be all spiffed up with new chairs and a brighter atmosphere.

Regardless of the surroundings, I always enjoy the food here. There are abundant seafood dishes such as beet-cured salmon with wasabi tobiko (fish roe), albacore tuna tataki with seaweed salad and pickled shiitake mushrooms, and lobster salad rolls with pickled carrots and a citrus Thai dressing. You'll also find sweet soy-marinated hanger steak in a Korean chili sauce, Vietnamese-style braised beef short ribs, spicy chicken wings with green onions and toasted almonds, and a big burger topped with kimchi and spiced tomato jam. My mouth is watering as I write.

Raw Bar has moved more strongly to the Asian side of things since Yellow Door opened in early 2013 to cover off Hotel Arts' breakfast, lunch and dinner obligations. That shift allows Raw Bar to focus on a narrower menu, a shift that helps them do what they do so well. Inside or out. (But I still like sitting by the pool best.)

**Address**
119 – 12 Avenue SW
(Hotel Arts)

**Phone**
403.206.9565

**Hours**
May – September:
Daily
Noon – late

October – April:
Daily
4:30 pm – late

**Reservations**
Accepted

**Cards**
V, MC, AE, Debit

**Drinks**
Full bar
No corkage

**Outdoor Dining**
Poolside patio

**Noise**
🔊 – 🔊))

**Price Range**
$$ – $$$

**Website**
hotelarts.ca

# Rea's

Italian

**M**ONA Lisa has been found!
Following a devastating fire at Rea's Italian Cucina in 2009 (same owners, but it was then called Sandro Pizzeria), only two things were recovered: the pizza oven and a framed print of the Mona Lisa. The pizza oven makes sense—it was accustomed to high temperatures. But Mona? She's flammable.

Curiously, though, during Rea's big reno and expansion after the blaze, Mona went missing. So when Rea's reopened only eight months later, there was a gap for regulars used to gazing upon Mona. But oddly—like the real Mona Lisa—she showed up a couple of years later, having been recovered by the salvage company.

In the meantime, Rea's had re-established itself as one of Calgary's premier pizza parlours and Italian restaurants. So there's a long list of pastas and veal dishes to accompany the equally long list of pizzas. We like the Dom Special, the pizza with mushrooms and crisp pancetta. (It comes with shrimp, too, but we leave them off. Besides, we've been known to share the linguine pittore with prosciutto and shrimp to start.)

Rea's is built for large family functions and lively meals for everyone. Quiet and romantic, it is not. If you're dining as a couple, you can easily be surrounded by raucous birthdays or soccer celebrations. That's part of the fun.

So is finding it. Located in the light industrial area of Edmonton Trail, this busy place is tucked between Wheel Pro's and a Rona outlet, giving it a hidden-gem kind of quality.

Just keep an eye out for Mona. We don't want her to go missing again.

**Address**
431 – 41 Avenue NE

**Phone**
403.230.7754

**Hours**
Monday – Friday
11 am – 2 pm

Monday – Saturday
5 pm – 10 pm

**Reservations**
Highly recommended

**Cards**
V, MC, AE, Debit

**Drinks**
Full bar
No corkage

**Outdoor Dining**
None

**Noise**
◁) – ◁))

**Price Range**
$$ – $$$

**Website**
reasrestaurant.com

# The Rimrock

Local Canadian

**F**OR pure history, no other Calgary restaurant comes close to the Rimrock in the Fairmont Palliser hotel. Since 1914 when the Palliser opened, there's been some kind of food service operation in this location. So it's seen every oil boom and bust Calgary has experienced, opening almost simultaneously as it did with the first well in Turner Valley. It's seen young people go off to too many wars and has hosted royalty, movie stars, Olympic heroes and visitors from around the globe.

Sit at one of the tables in front of the Rimrock's fireplace and you have a good chance of sharing your spot with the ghost of R.B. Bennett, Canada's Depression-era Prime Minister. (He lived for a time in room 760 and sat at one of the fireplace tables to open his morning mail.) Stroll to the back of the room and gaze upon Charlie Beil's rimrock mural. Run your hands over the fine-tooled leather-clad pillars placed throughout the room. (Why not? Everyone does.)

And enjoy the food, a globally inspired, locally sourced collection of dishes that ranges from salmon-belly tartare and Thai lobster bisque (all of the Rimrock's seafood is Ocean Wise-certified) to a 14-ounce bone-in rib-eye with roasted wild mushrooms and an angel food cake with berries and a strawberry drizzle.

That's just a sampling of the dinner menu. The Rimrock covers all the bases for the hotel, from breakfast through lunch to dinner. They also do a seasonal Death By Chocolate event and a Sunday brunch buffet. The Rimrock is one busy joint.

Which just helps it keep making Calgary history.

**Address**
133 – 9 Avenue SW
(The Fairmont Palliser)

**Phone**
403.260.1219

**Hours**
Daily
6:30 am – 10:30 am
5:30 pm – 9 pm

Monday – Friday
11:30 am – 1:30 pm

Sunday
11 am – 1:30 pm

**Reservations**
Recommended

**Cards**
V, MC, AE, Debit

**Drinks**
Full bar
Corkage $25/bottle

**Outdoor Dining**
None

**Noise**
◁ – ◁)

**Price Range**
$$$ – $$$$

**Website**
fairmont.com/palliser

downtown calgary

# River Café

RIVER Café has been clobbered by two floods within a decade. The first one, back in 2005, knocked out their water and sewage system for months; the second, the 2013 behemoth, took a toll on their basement, washing out their wine cellar and charcuterie aging room. (No, there were no bargain deals on label-less wines—they all had to be destroyed.)

But Sal Howell and her beloved River Café keep coming back. Less than two months after the 2013 flood, they were up and running, with enough summer remaining to allow for some lazy days on the gorgeous patio. Initially built to be a City Parks concession stand, River Café has substantial concrete moorings. And it's located on a bit of a rise, so the main floor, with its open kitchen and its bentwood, lodgy accoutrements, has—touch wood—never been dampened. River Café is resilient, as are its staff and its many fans.

I'm always impressed at how the kitchen staff can turn humble, local ingredients, such as nettles, lentils, canola seeds and Swiss chard, into gourmet feasts. Plates might include wild boar tenderloin with grilled Okanagan peaches, cornbread purée, arugula, local goat feta and green beans or perhaps Noble Farms duck with smoked-apple bread pudding or maybe Ocean Wise sturgeon with sea urchin potage and confit potato. The menu changes with the season, so the offerings could be a surprise.

So could the prices. Entrees are in the mid-$30s to mid-$40s. This kind of food doesn't come cheap. So be prepared. But it's so local, so good and so water-resistant, it's a perennial favourite.

**Address**
Prince's Island Park

**Phone**
403.261.7670

**Hours**
May – September:
Monday – Friday
11 am – 11 pm

Saturday & Sunday
10 am – 11 pm

October – April:
Monday – Friday
11 am – 10 pm

Saturday & Sunday
10 am – 10 pm

(Closed in January)

**Reservations**
Highly recommended

**Cards**
V, MC, AE, Debit

**Drinks**
Full bar
Corkage $20/bottle
Free corkage Sundays

**Outdoor Dining**
Patio

**Noise**
◁) – ◁))

**Price Range**
$$$ – $$$$

**Website**
river-cafe.com

downtown
calgary

# Rouge

French-Influenced
Regional

**Address**
1240 – 8 Avenue SE

**Phone**
403.531.2767

**Hours**
Monday – Friday
11:30 am – 2 pm

Monday – Saturday
5 pm – close

**Reservations**
Recommended

**Cards**
V, MC, AE, Debit

**Drinks**
Full bar
No corkage

**Outdoor Dining**
Patio

**Noise**
◁) – ◁))

**Price Range**
$$$ – $$$$

**Website**
rougecalgary.com

IN my books, exquisite cooking is about making something very complex seem simple and elevating the simple to new heights. Nowhere in this book will you find that done better than at Rouge. That's right, I'm calling out Rouge as the Number One restaurant in this book.

Why not? Partners Paul Rogalski and Olivier Reynaud have built Rouge and its reputation from the ground up, from the scant early days in 2001 to the robust mini-empire that now includes the also-excellent Bistro Rouge.

How do they do it so well? Rogalski concentrates on the kitchen, guiding a team that can sear foie gras and combine it with rhubarb compote (concocted with stalks from their own garden), pain perdu and dandelion honey pearls (the dandelions also being from the yard). They can cook a lamb loin to a dreamy medium rare and combine it with smashed chickpeas and merguez sausage in a Moroccan turn, then plop a minted hollandaise on top. And they can smoke a pork chop so it's still juicy (a kitchen that really knows how to do pork!) and side it with lusciously creamy grits and a mustard jus. Simple. Complex. Impeccable.

There's the setting, too—the historic Cross House and its yard that goes on forever, allowing them to have a great garden. And the service staff, who know just how good the food is and work under one of the best—Olivier Reynaud. (Reynaud is also responsible for the outstanding wine list.)

This is why Rouge made it onto the San Pellegrino list of the world's top restaurants in 2010. And why it's the top restaurant in this book. Simple.

# Rush | Evolved Steakhouse

**B**IRTHED in late 2008 at the start of the last recession, Rush has been challenged from the beginning with finding its rightful place in the culinary firmament. Which is a shame. It's had excellent food from the get-go from a succession of excellent chefs. The room is gorgeous and the kitchen is one of the best equipped in town. But the location—in the former main post office west of the Palliser—is just enough off the Stephen Avenue path to miss the heavy diner traffic.

Still, Rush has hung in there, and as I was completing this book, it was about to undergo a makeover. The carpeted, high-ceilinged dining room was to become "bolder" and more "masculine," and the menu was to hew away from global inspirations and move closer to a contemporary steakhouse. As executive chef Andrew Keen said, "It'll still be Rush, but it'll be the 2013 model instead of the 2008 one."

I'm told the new model will retain items such as the tasty and seriously aged (as in 55 days) beef strip loins and introduce seafood dishes like lobster pot pie. And here's hoping they honour their promise to keep the butter cake on the dessert list. This is one of the best desserts in the city, a round, creamy cake topped with crème anglaise and fresh fruit. Served for two, it's capable of satisfying four. (Not that there isn't a certain family member who'd like to hog a whole one for herself.)

So I anxiously anticipate the new Rush, hoping it's as good as the old one.

**Address**
100, 207– 9 Avenue SW

**Phone**
403.271.7874

**Hours**
Dining Room:
Monday – Friday
11:30 am – 2:30 pm

Monday – Saturday
5 pm – 9:30 pm

Lounge:
Monday – Friday
11:30 am – close

Saturday
5 pm – close

**Reservations**
Recommended

**Cards**
V, MC, AE, Debit

**Drinks**
Full bar
No corkage

**Outdoor Dining**
None

**Noise**
◁ – ◁»

**Price Range**
$$$ – $$$$

**Website**
rushrestaurant.com

downtown calgary

# Sabroso

## Nuevo Latino

REMEMBER Mescalero? That big, fire-damaged building on 1st Street SW that looked more like a Santa Fe restaurant than any Sante Fe restaurant? The place that had a big wood-burning oven and looked gorgeous in summer and winter, at night or in broad daylight? And served fine Southwestern food? It's gone, but it's not forgotten.

When brothers Alejandro and Orlando Morante were opening Sabroso, they called upon Mescalero owner and designer Witold Twardowski to assist with the look. The result is a dark-toned, concrete-floored space lit by pounded-tin, star-shaped lamps and decorated with Latin American memorabilia. Sabroso is a mini-Mescalero in spirit.

In flavour, it takes off with Nuevo Latino cuisine, a style that draws from the traditions of Latin America but adjusts with European technique and global ingredients. So you'll find a Japanese-influenced Peruvian tiradito of soy- and morita chili-marinated albacore tuna and Venezuelan arepas stuffed with chicken, beef, pulled pork or portobello mushrooms. From Argentina, there's a chimichurri-sauced steak sided with sprouted quinoa, and from Cuba, there are multi-layered sandwiches.

The almejas al vapor ($11)—a Peruvian clam stew with shrimp, chorizo, roast corn and dumpling-like pan de yuca—is outstanding with rich, creamy flavours jumping around. The tiradito ($12) is a flavour parade of tuna, soy, smoked chilies and pickled vegetables—a challenge for your palate to sort out. This is terrific food.

Throw in the live salsa music and you have a new destination for the Latin American crowd and aficionados—a fine replacement for Mescalero.

**Address**
1504 – 16 Avenue SW

**Phone**
587.350.2679

**Hours**
Tuesday – Thursday
11 am – 10 pm

Friday & Saturday
11 am – 2 am

Sunday
11 am – 6 pm

**Reservations**
Recommended

**Cards**
V, MC, AE, Debit

**Drinks**
Full bar
Corkage $15/bottle

**Outdoor Dining**
Patio

**Noise**
◁) – ◁))

**Price Range**
$$ – $$$

**Website**
sabrosos.ca

# Safari Grill | East African Indian

SAFARI Grill is an East African Indian restaurant and its cuisine comes from the culture of Indian people who moved to Kenya and Tanzania over a century ago. So it's offering something quite different for Calgary restaurant goers.

You'll find chicken mishkaki, kebabs marinated in a chili-rich pili pili sauce, and a deep-fried cassava dish with more pili pili sauce. And there's kuku paka, chicken in coconut curry. These are Indian-influenced East African dishes seldom found in India itself. But you can get them at Safari Grill, along with a long list of curries and vegetarian dishes and barbecued meats. It's a wide-reaching menu.

In a unique setting, too. Safari Grill is a glassed-in space seating about 60 and draped in zebra prints—on the walls, on the tabletops and on the seats. Completing the safari ambience are African pictures, mementos and music. And that food.

The menu presents many dishes as individual meals with rice and bread, unlike most Indian restaurants where you order dishes for sharing. (You can still share at Safari Grill, which we did.) We started with some tasty kachori, little pastry balls made from lentil dough and filled with puréed lentils. They're fried and served with a variety of chutneys and sauces. I liked the tamarind sauce on them, but the lime pickle was good too. Then we had a smooth and gentle eggplant and potato dish with rice and chapati, and the intensely flavoured Masai goat with rice and roti. Both were great.

Sadly, we missed that kuku paka. Next time.

**Address**
225 – 28 Street SE
(Short Pants Plaza)

**Phone**
403.235.6655

**Hours**
Tuesday – Thursday
11:30 am – 10 pm

Friday
11:30 am – 11 pm

Saturday
1 pm – 11 pm

Sunday
2 pm – 10 pm

**Reservations**
Accepted

**Cards**
V, MC, Debit

**Drinks**
Full bar
Corkage $7/bottle

**Outdoor Dining**
Patio

**Noise**
◁)

**Price Range**
$$ – $$$

**Website**
safarigrillcalgary.com

# Sage Bistro

Contemporary
Canadian

**Address**
1712 Bow Valley Trail
Canmore

**Phone**
403.678.4878

**Hours**
Dining Room:
Monday – Friday
11:30 am – 10 pm

Saturday & Sunday
10 am – 10 pm

Wine Lounge:
Monday – Friday
5 pm – 11 pm

Saturday & Sunday
3 pm – 11 pm

**Reservations**
Recommended for
dining room
Accepted in lounge for
groups of 6 or more

**Cards**
V, MC, Debit

**Drinks**
Full bar
Corkage $20/bottle in
dining room only

**Outdoor Dining**
3 decks

**Noise**
◁ – ◁))

**Price Range**
$$ – $$$

**Website**
sagebistro.ca

I BREATHED a sigh of relief when I saw Sage Bistro's menu a few years ago. After expanding the log building by adding a large wine lounge on the top floor, I was concerned that Sage might mess around with the dining room food. Sage, you see, is my mother-in-law's favourite Canmore restaurant, and their rosemary- and port-braised lamb shank ($27) has been her favourite dish for a long time. Add to that my father-in-law's favourite dish—the Thai curry bowl with chicken and prawns ($26)—and you could easily have a recipe for disaster if you dropped these.

Fortunately, Sage owner Todd Kunst is a savvy hombre. He's kept both dishes on the dining room menu, along with the popular seafood risotto and the Sylvan Star Gouda-laced mac'n'cheese. And he's created a whole new menu for the wine lounge.

Sage keeps over 250 wines in stock, with over 20 available by the glass. And the wine lounge menu has been developed to complement your beverage choices. There's beef tartare (big reds), a Caprese salad (Pinot Grigio, perhaps) using Calgary's White Gold fior di latte cheese, steamed mussels (Sauvignon Blanc) and ginger-beef lettuce wraps (Cabernet Sauvignon). There's an antipasto platter and a selection of charcuterie, including many from local favourite, Valbella Gourmet Foods. There's also a half dozen or so gelatos and sorbets and an upscale version of s'mores featuring smoked, house-made marshmallow and a Belgian chocolate ganache.

Sage's food is robust and full-bodied, all house-prepared and served with a smile. I've always found service here to be friendly and efficient, respectful and attentive. Which can bring on another sigh of relief.

# Santorini | Greek

**W**HENEVER I'm in need of a little island time, Greek-style, I head to Santorini for their Taverna Special. That's a multi-course menu of mezethes (Greek small plates) that includes many of Santorini's highlights.

The meal, for two or more, starts slowly with hummus, saganaki (the flamed cheese), warm pita and horiatiki salad. Something smooth, something crunchy, something salty and something warm. Nice. Then it builds with crisp calamari, hearty keftedes (beef meatballs), and spanakopita (spinach and cheese wrapped in phyllo pastry and baked). Things get more serious when their arni kleftiko—roast lamb, falling off the bone—appears. Roasted potatoes are laid alongside it, and lemon wedges are at the ready to squeeze over both lamb and spuds. Gorgeous lamb, great potatoes.

Somewhere along the line, a good bottle of red Greek wine, the perfect foil for the food, will be opened. I'll have settled into the whitewashed plaster interior, listening to the bouzouki music and dreaming about the Mediterranean.

I've been indulging here since 1986 when Andreas and Maria Nicolaides opened Santorini, providing me this brief escape from reality by serving up flocks of lamb, oceans of calamari and lively Greek hospitality (plus a few ouzos). They've renovated recently, giving Santorini a refreshed look. It still has the patina of a Greek taverna that's been washed ashore on Centre Street, but it seems brighter, and somehow, the food tastes even better.

Santorini is a classic—a sincere owner-run restaurant that is as consistent as you can get. That's why I rely on it for my island time.

**Address**
1502 Centre Street N

**Phone**
403.276.8363

**Hours**
Tuesday – Thursday
11 am – 10 pm

Friday
11 am – 11 pm

Saturday
Noon – 11 pm

Sunday
4 pm – 10 pm

**Reservations**
Recommended

**Cards**
V, MC, AE, Debit

**Drinks**
Full bar
Corkage $20/bottle

**Outdoor Dining**
Patio

**Noise**
◁) – ◁))

**Price Range**
$$ – $$$

**Website**
santorinirestaurant.com

# Shigatsu

**Japanese Fusion**

**W**HEN Shigatsu opened, the owner differentiated it from the sushi crowd by calling it a Japanese fusion restaurant and creating a menu that keys on cooked dishes. Things like stir-fried chicken in a spicy miso sauce, slow-cooked pork belly with a secret Okinawa-style sauce and grilled salmon neck with a savoury blend of seasonings. There are tempuras and teriyakis and a few salads, too, including a sashimi one tossed with fresh greens in a spicy vinaigrette. This is interesting stuff.

Shigatsu has sushi—really good sushi—but they also serve the best gyoza dumplings I've had. They're light and tender and packed with flavour, even without the dipping sauce, which is also light and flavourful. The crusted rock prawns served with a chili-spiked mayo are great too—six of them served hot and crunchy.

Of course, I have tried some sushi, both rolls and nigiri. Beautifully cut, expertly rolled, excellent flavours and textures. The rice could be zippier, but is still quite acceptable. I would rank them in the top tier of local sushi places.

I'm also impressed with the space. It previously housed another Japanese place called Gunkan. Back then, it was a large open room decorated mostly in brown. Shigatsu has been filled with booths and private dining areas, decorated with crystals and tones of black with a bit of red.

So I like what Shigatsu has done. They've managed to create a Japanese restaurant that is different from the masses of other ones and that's a good thing.

**Address**
3106 – 4 Street NW

**Phone**
403.800.0567

**Hours**
Wednesday – Monday
11:30 am – 2 pm
5 pm – 9:30 pm

**Reservations**
Accepted

**Cards**
V, MC, Debit

**Drinks**
Full bar
Corkage $10/bottle
or $5/person

**Outside Dining**
Patio in 2014

**Noise**
◁ – ◁))

**Price Range**
$$ – $$$

**Website**
No

# Shikiji

## Japanese (Noodles & Sushi)

**Address**
1608 Centre Street N

**Phone**
403.520.0093

**Hours**
Daily
11:30 am – 1:45 pm
5 pm – 8:45 pm

**Reservations**
Recommended

**Cards**
V, MC, AE, Debit

**Drinks**
Full bar
Corkage $10/bottle

**Outdoor Dining**
None

**Noise**
◁ – ◁»

**Price Range**
$$

**Website**
shikiji.ca

O F the many Japanese restaurants in this book, most focus on sushi, albeit with a menu of cooked Japanese dishes, too. But there are also a few Japanese noodle houses in here, featuring ramen (thin wheat-flour noodles), udon (thick wheat-flour noodles) or soba (buckwheat) noodles.

At Shikiji, they do all three kinds in a mind-boggling variety of flavour combos like miso or soy ramen; chicken or tempura udon; ten zaru soba served cold with a quail egg and tempura or Shikiji soba served hot with a kitchen sink of ingredients.

I like the chili-goma ramen that comes in a huge bowl with two spoons, one for sipping the broth, the other, slotted for scooping the spicy ground pork out of the broth. There are chopsticks, too, for lifting the noodles. This is a fine bowl of soup filled with textures, from the ground pork and noodles to the crunchy green onions and smooth shiitake mushrooms. And there's a serious spice-bite with a nutty sesame flavour, too.

If you'd like to add to your noodle fix, or avoid one all together, Shikiji does have some fine sushi—as well-conceived and executed as at any place in town.

I enjoy the Shikiji space, too. A small square room, it has many private corners in which to enjoy your meal, with a short sushi bar and a scenic corner bar overlooking the frightfully close intersection of Centre Street and 16th Avenue N.

Note: At press time, Shikiji was in the process of opening Shiki, a small ramen-only spot on 1st Avenue NE in Bridgeland.

# Shiraz | Persian

**P**ARTLY it's the uniqueness of the flavours that draws me to Persian food. Combining ingredients like pomegranate molasses and ground walnuts with chicken is a great taste sensation. But it's as much about the texture as the taste for me. Add crispy onions to the above mix and it becomes crunchy and creamy at the same time.

Much of Persian food is smooth and creamy (think roasted eggplant mixed with whey), while other dishes are pure meat (the various beef, lamb and chicken kebabs). But there's always a variation of texture to keep the mouth interested.

At Shiraz, I'm tempted to order the Tour of Persia combo to try as much variation as possible. The Tour, which admittedly is built for three people, contains three kebabs (beef strip loin, ground beef and chicken), the stew of the day (maybe eggplant or okra or the pomegranate-chicken one), zereshk polo (a rice dish filled with dried barberries, which have a vague similarity to dried cranberries), plus saffron-tinged basmati, peppers and onions. A great feast.

The Shiraz space is conducive to relaxed dining. Large black leather booths wrap around you, and subdued lighting softens the mood. Deep red walls and Persian decorations add to the tone.

Shiraz is family run by professionals who have been in the business for years. So service is seamless and well timed, the food is abundant and tasty, and the welcome is warm and sincere. Shiraz, named after one of the great cities of Persia, provides texture in the experience as well as the food. (And save room for the saffron ice cream.)

**Address**
1120 Centre Street N

**Phone**
403.452.4050

**Hours**
Monday
4:30 pm – 10 pm

Tuesday – Thursday, Sunday
11:30 am – 10 pm

Friday & Saturday
11:30 am – 11 pm

**Reservations**
Accepted

**Cards**
V, MC, Debit

**Drinks**
Full bar
Corkage $15/bottle

**Outdoor Dining**
None

**Noise**
◁)

**Price Range**
$$ – $$$

**Website**
shirazpersiancuisine.ca

# Silver Dragon

Chinese (Cantonese, Peking, Szechuan)

**T**ALK about variety. From a soup of seafood and bamboo to braised abalone in oyster sauce, Silver Dragon has over 250 dishes on its regular list. Add in banquet menus, special dishes for traditional diners and dim sum (in the Calgary location) and you have two fine, all-purpose places for Chinese food fans.

Cruising on to nearly a half-century in Calgary, Silver Dragon still commands the same second-floor Chinatown location. It's huge and seems perpetually packed, but there's almost always room somewhere for a hungry group. (Unless, that is, you show up without a reservation in the heat of the weekend dim sum brunch. You'll be waiting awhile then.) The Banff spot, around for a quarter-century now, is a black and red, third-floor room with a great mountain view.

Silver Dragon's large menu keys on traditional Cantonese and modern Hong Kong dishes, so many of the flavours tend to be mild and natural. Dishes like lemon chicken, pineapple sweet and sour pork, and chicken chop suey appear at both locations, along with black pepper shredded-beef hot plates and pine-nut prawns with creamy butter sauce. But the selection reaches into other areas of China, too, such as Szechuan and Hunan, adding zip and intensity to some dishes. And, of course, there's ginger beef in a nod to their Calgary hometown.

Service at both Silver Dragons is brisk and efficient. Don't expect abundant niceties here; instead, expect food hot and fresh from the kitchen, served professionally and priced accordingly. (Very few dishes, even the seafood, break the $20 mark.)

**Address**
106 – 3 Avenue SE

**Phone**
403.264.5326

**Hours**
Monday – Thursday
10 am – 11:30 pm

Friday & Saturday
9:30 am – 12:30 am

Sunday & Holidays
9 am – 10:30 pm

 downtown calgary

---

**Address**
211 Banff Avenue
Banff

**Phone**
403.762.3939

**Hours**
Daily
11:30 am – 10 pm

**Outdoor Dining**
Deck

---

**Common Info**

**Reservations**
Recommended

**Cards**
V, MC, AE, Debit

**Drinks**
Full bar
No corkage

**Noise**
◁) – ◁))

**Price Range**
$ – $$$

**Website**
None

# Silver Inn

I FINALLY broke out of the box.

Usually, when I visit Silver Inn, I don't even look at the menu. Since 1975, my go-to dishes have always been grilled dumplings, chicken and cashews in yellow bean sauce, and ginger beef. I can't help myself. Since I was introduced to these dishes at Silver Inn those many years ago, they've been my standard for this style of Peking (Beijing) food.

But I thought it was time for a change. So instead of the chicken, this time I looked at the menu and ordered stir-fried prawns and vegetables in a black bean sauce. That meant I could order ginger chicken instead of ginger beef. (OK, not such a big change, but still...) And instead of the grilled dumplings, I ordered, well, the grilled dumplings.

I like change but only so much at a time, please. And those dumplings are always so good, made fresh daily with light overtones of green onion and ginger, grilled to smoking-hot perfection. (I've frequently written about how hot from the wok Silver Inn's food is.) In an age of frozen, factory-made dumplings, these continue to be a revelation.

Which is also the word to describe the prawns in black bean sauce: a revelation. Great quality, loads of prawns, crunchy vegetables, silky-thick sauce. Lovely. And that ginger chicken? Boneless chunks (deboned in-house for quality control), lightly battered and coated with their gingery, peppery sauce. It almost made me forget about the ginger beef.

But not forever. Next time I may well go back to my original three dishes. And I'll be happy about it.

**Address**
2702 Centre Street N

**Phone**
403.276.6711

**Hours**
Tuesday – Friday
11 am – 2 pm

Tuesday – Sunday
5 pm – 10 pm

**Reservations**
Recommended

**Cards**
V, MC, AE, Debit

**Drinks**
Full bar
Free corkage

**Outdoor Dining**
None

**Noise**
◁ – ◁))

**Price Range**
$$

**Website**
silverinnrestaurant.com

# Sky 360

Contemporary
Canadian

**B**EEN meaning to look the new Bow building in the eye? Want to take a gander at the downtown parking situation with a bird's eye view? Got some relatives in town chomping to see the sights? You know where to go: up the Calgary Tower to Sky 360.

High-altitude restaurants offer many a challenge to a chef. In the case of Sky 360, the kitchen is locked into the same dimensions it had when built to celebrate Canada's centennial in 1967. There's not much room for expansion at 191 metres up, no room for decent wine storage and little for any high-tech kitchen equipment. And it helps if your kitchen staff is short.

Yet Sky 360 remains a constant draw for visitors and locals alike. The view is spectacular, even if some new structures (hear that, Bow building?) take up a lot of space. I particularly like going for breakfast or brunch (although these days, it's only offered Sundays). Or later in the day, when the sun is settling behind the Rockies.

The food at Sky 360 is an eclectic mix of bruschetta, Caesar salad, crab cakes, fettuccine carbonara, a short rib sandwich and steelhead trout. It's part comfort food, part contemporary, created to appeal to the broad market that visits the tower.

Food and service are usually quite good, but prices are a little higher than they should be ($38 for lamb shank at dinner? $22 for blackened ling cod fish 'n' chips at lunch?). At least the elevation fee is included with the purchase of an entree. And that view is priceless.

**Address**
101 – 9 Avenue SW
(Calgary Tower)

**Phone**
403.532.7966

**Hours**
Monday – Saturday
11 am – 2 pm

Sunday
10 am – 2 pm

Daily
5 pm – close

**Reservations**
Highly recommended

**Cards**
V, MC, AE, Debit

**Drinks**
Full bar
No corkage

**Outdoor Dining**
None

**Noise**
◁ – ◁»

**Price Range**
$$$ – $$$$

**Website**
sky360.ca

downtown
calgary

# Sleeping Buffalo

**T**HE elk horn chandelier gets me every time. Buffalo Mountain Lodge has just the right tone of mountain rusticity and class, epitomized by that big elk horn chandelier hanging over the lounge. It's by the riverstone fireplace, the one with the bison head mounted over it. Yes, this is a mountain lodge of the highest order.

And the Sleeping Buffalo dining room continues the theme with a wraparound view of its Tunnel Mountain surroundings. For those looking for a quieter spot away from the Banff Avenue crowds and with a sense-surround of nature, this is it. Sleeping Buffalo—which, by the way, is the traditional Native name for Tunnel Mountain since that is what it resembles—covers the breakfast, lunch and dinner necessities for the lodge. (Cilantro, with its great patio, also offers summer-season options.)

Lunch is a favourite here, if only because the view is better in sunlight. Both lunch and dinner include a number of Canadian Rocky Mountain Resorts' meat products such as smoked buffalo and elk salami. And dinner reaches into elk strip loin and Alberta lamb territory.

I wanted to try the elk ham, so opted for the lunchtime elk-ham Reuben with Appenzeller cheese and house-made sauerkraut. Nicely flavoured elk ham—almost a pastrami style, but drier than a pork version. (Not off-puttingly dry; just drier than regular ham.) A nice sandwich ($17). I had it with a side of roasted cauliflower soup topped with an aged cheddar crouton. Excellent rendition of cauliflower.

And walking in to that chandelier gets me every time.

## Address
Tunnel Mountain Road
(Buffalo Mountain Lodge)
Banff

## Phone
403.760.4484

## Hours
Dining Room:
Daily
7 am – 11:30 am
Noon – 3 pm
6 pm – 9 pm

Lounge:
Daily
3 pm – 6 pm

(Check for seasonal variation)

## Reservations
Accepted for dinner
Not accepted for lounge

## Cards
V, MC, AE, Debit

## Drinks
Full bar
No corkage

## Outdoor Dining
None

## Noise
◁ – ◁))

## Price Range
$$ – $$$

## Website
crmr.com

# Spice 7

**M**IRCHI has been a landmark of local Pakistani cuisine since 2007. The only problem is how tricky it can be to snag one of the 16 seats shoehorned into the space.

So a few years after opening, owner Amjad Shehzad leased a larger location downtown and opened a second Mirchi. But seeking to differentiate it from the original, he recently renamed it Spice 7. Same richly seasoned and sauced foods, same kebabs, same roasted tikka dishes and karahis (stews named after the pot they're cooked in). But a whole lot more room.

And a lovely room at that. Shehzad brought in silver-tinged wood furniture, ceramic tiles, glass-topped tables and ornate decorations from Pakistan. The result is one of the prettiest restaurants in town.

In addition to offering the traditional menu at Spice 7, he also serves entrees that look like Western plates, with a protein, a starch and a vegetable. So when you order the halibut masala ($22) or the tamarind-demerara marinated beef tenderloin with black cumin curry ($24), your plate will also include basmati rice and a vegetarian selection such as aloo gobhi (curried potato and cauliflower) or kaala channa (black chickpea curry). He even does a beef rib steak drenched in spices. (Be sure to mention if you'd like your beef cooked less than well done though. That's the standard here.) A special treat are the basa fish pakoras, lightly coated in chickpea batter and fried. Served hot and crisp with tamarind sauce and raita, they're a great appetizer.

It's so nice to enjoy this food in the spacious, relaxing confines of Spice 7. Finally, elbow room at last.

**Address**
739 – 2 Avenue SW

**Phone**
587.353.0733

**Hours**
Monday – Friday
11:30 am – 2 pm

Sunday – Thursday
5 pm – 10 pm

Friday & Saturday
5 pm – 11 pm

**Reservations**
Recommended

**Cards**
V, MC, Debit

**Drinks**
No alcoholic beverages

**Outdoor Dining**
None

**Noise**
🔊

**Price Range**
$ – $$$

**Website**
spice7.ca

downtown
calgary

---

**Other Location**

Mirchi
825 – 12 Avenue SW
403.245.3663
mirchirest.com

# Spolumbo's

Italian Deli & Sausage Makers

**Address**
1308 – 9 Avenue SE

**Phone**
403.264.6452

**Hours**
Monday – Saturday
8 am – 5:30 pm

**Reservations**
Accepted for private room only

**Cards**
V, MC, AE, Debit

**Drinks**
Beer & wine
No corkage

**Outdoor Dining**
Patio

**Noise**
◁) – ◁))

**Price Range**
$ – $$

**Website**
spolumbos.com

It's a Monday when I show up at Spolumbo's. What am I thinking? Sure the lineup is shorter than most other days (especially Friday), but there's no special on Monday. Wednesday, it's turkey meat loaf (man, that's good); Saturday, it's porchetta (damn, that's even better); and Thursday through Saturday, it's the regular meat loaf (so good they had to expand it to three days). I rely on the specials at Spolumbo's. It takes the anxiety out of ordering. "Just give me the special" I'll say, like I'm a regular with no worries in the world.

But today, it's Monday. No special. I start to sweat.

OK, I can do this. How about a nice Italian panini layered with cold cuts and cheeses? Or a nice bowl of soup with a salad? Where's my head? Salad? At Spolumbo's? Get a grip, man. Breathe.

Then, as Dean Martin sings "When the moon hits your eye like a big pizza pie," it dawns on me. A meatball sandwich! Yes! On a crusty Italian roll slathered in tomato sauce. That's the answer.

So I order, I sit, I devour—splashes of sauce threatening my clean shirt. I relax into the surroundings of hungry folks scarfing back sandwiches and sausages. I gaze at the framed sports jerseys hanging on the walls—Heatley, DeAngelis, Ovechkin—nice collection. I demolish the sandwich, creating a pile of messy napkins in the process. I'm relieved and relaxed.

Then one of the Spolumbo guys stops by: "Have you tried our Italian-spiced beef and pork burgers yet?"

Argghh. Why do they do this to me?

# Sugo | Italian

"**W**E just call it Italian," says co-owner Jesse Johnson, describing the food at Sugo.

It seems like such a simple label for such a creative menu that included grilled coho salmon with a spicy mango caponata and house-smoked pork loin with fall-down-good smoked apples and onions last time we ate there. The grilled prawns—in an escarole salad with White Gold fior di latte mozzarella and marinated artichoke hearts in lemon vinaigrette—were declared by Catherine to be the most perfect prawns she'd had in Calgary.

Sure, there are more traditional Italian dishes like gnocchi, but the little potato flour dumplings come with house-smoked bacon, leeks and a veal-prawn involtini. Sugo has nice ideas, beautiful preparations and menus that change daily. Johnson and business partner/executive chef Angelo Contrada, who have run the Inglewood restaurant since the early 2000s, have always strode beyond the red-checkered tablecloth style, offering dishes with a more contemporary tone.

The room itself could be any kind of contemporary restaurant with its high ceiling and two long, narrow spaces, one for the dining room, one for the lounge. A bar along the end helps anchor the space, forming it into a horseshoe. It's all in an old building with a charming patina of age, but is still fresh and light. Folded napkins create individual place settings, and basil plants adorned tables when we were there.

Sugo's staff provide personalized, confident service. This is a restaurant that is consistent and shows its maturity—in spite of the menu being created daily, the staff know the dishes, their ingredients and their quality.

Just Italian, indeed.

**Address**
1214 – 9 Avenue SE

**Phone**
403.263.1115

**Hours**
Monday
5 pm – close

Tuesday – Friday
11 am – close

Saturday
5 pm – close

**Reservations**
Recommended

**Cards**
V, MC, AE, Debit

**Drinks**
Full bar
Corkage $20/bottle

**Outdoor Dining**
None

**Noise**

**Price Range**
$$ – $$$$

**Website**
sugo.ca

# Sultan's Tent

Moroccan

**T**HE trickiest thing about Sultan's Tent is finding it. You'd think a restaurant hugging 14th Street would be easy to spot. But no. Located just north of the 14th Street bridge and just south of that other culinary landmark—Chicken on the Way—Sultan's Tent can be maddeningly invisible to many who buzz by looking for it.

Once you've found it, though, you'll be wrapped in its cocoon of Moroccan warmth. Low, cushioned benches surround large brass tables. Detailed weavings and carpets hang as room dividers, and blue cloth is draped overhead to replicate a tent. Sink into the cushions and relax. Let the space transport you to North Africa.

You can order a couscous or tajine from the long list (lamb, chicken, merguez, prawn, vegetarian and so on) or simply opt for a "feast," either the Sultan's or the Sultana's. Both include the tangy harira soup, the choice of a briq (phyllo-wrapped meats or vegetables) or the b'stilla, a couscous or tajine, dessert, and mint tea or Moroccan coffee. (The Sultana's feast has a half portion of the main course.)

Although the briqs are tempting, the b'stilla is one of the most unique—and tasty—dishes of any culture. Chicken, eggs, almonds and seasonings are wrapped in phyllo, baked and then topped with icing sugar and cinnamon. Crisp, sweet, savoury and fragrant, it's a flavour and texture combination that works fascinatingly well. By the way, you eat all this with the fingers of your right hand (cutlery optional).

And now that you've found Sultan's Tent, next time will be easier.

**Address**
4 – 14 Street NW

**Phone**
403.244.2333

**Hours**
Wednesday – Sunday
5 pm – close

**Reservations**
Recommended

**Cards**
V, MC, AE, Debit

**Drinks**
Full bar
No corkage

**Outdoor Dining**
None

**Noise**
◁ – ◁)

**Price Range**
$$$

**Website**
sultanstent.ca

# Sushi Club

As a young man in Japan, Koki Miyashita learned how to cook in a Western restaurant. He specialized in pizza, steak and ribs and even made a killer cheesecake. When he arrived in Canada in 1982, he had never sliced a single piece of sashimi. Everything he knows about sushi, he learned in Calgary.

Which is not to say his learning was anything less than excellent. Miyashita was a keen student under chef Shoji at the Sukiyaki House, and by 1988, he had risen to head sushi chef and trainer there.

When it was time to start his own restaurant, he called on Katsuye "Steve" Inoue—a former student of his—to join him as an equal partner. In 2003, they opened Sushi Club, where they have been slicing and dicing hamachi, tuna and smoked steelhead ever since. They've built a reputation as two of the best sushi chefs in the city, a pair seasoned in the traditions of sushi, yet not afraid to innovate. Take, for example, the prosciutto-mango roll that includes smoked steelhead, smoked black cod, wasabi tobiko and cream cheese. Creative stuff.

Sushi is the stock-in-trade at Sushi Club, with over 90 percent of business coming from their maki, nigiri, cones and sashimi. All is made to order and individually formed—no sushi machines here. Miyashita and Inoue need to feel the rice and the fish to know how best to handle them.

As for the "club" part of the name, not to worry. Sushi Club requires no membership—they're open to anyone looking for well-made sushi.

**Address**
1240 Kensington Road NW

**Phone**
403.283.4100

**Hours**
Monday,
Wednesday – Friday
11:30 am – 2 pm

Sunday & Monday,
Wednesday & Thursday
5 pm – 9 pm

Friday & Saturday
5 pm – 9:30 pm

**Reservations**
Recommended

**Cards**
V, MC, AE, Debit

**Drinks**
Full bar
Corkage $18/bottle

**Outdoor Dining**
None

**Noise**
◁ – ◁)

**Price Range**
$$ – $$$

**Website**
No

# Szechuan Restaurant

Chinese (Szechuan)

**W**ow, this food is hot!

When you see a plate that's half covered in little red chili peppers, you know your taste buds are in for a scorching. And that's what Szechuan Restaurant is all about. After all, this is the food of Szechuan, which a chef from the area reminds me "is very hot because Szechuan is very cold." Got it.

It's a long menu of over 100 dishes with names like "crispy prawns with chili pepper," "stir-fried mussels in hot sauce" and "chicken in red chili sauce." You don't have to look hard to find spicy dishes; most are described similarly (including "duck in spicy Molson beer sauce").

Szechuan's food is also very tasty—given that it's hot. The Dandan noodles, a big bowl of noodles bathed in red chili sauce, are a fave. And the "crispy chicken" is just that—crisp, light and flavourful. (It's one of the few mild dishes on the menu.) Plates are abundantly filled and reasonably priced. Even the seafood dishes stay well under $20.

As for decor, this is a lovely space that needs serious work. It's the former Mamma's Ristorante/La Pasta spot that was so popular in the 1980s for its fine Italian cuisine and Mediterranean tone. Later in life, it became a sushi bar. Now, it's Szechuan. So it has overtones of Italian, Japanese and Chinese in the look. And like I said, it needs work.

But it doesn't matter so much when you're sweating your way through a meal here. You'll be focused on your taste buds.

**Address**
320 – 16 Avenue NW

**Phone**
403.276.8876

**Hours**
Monday – Friday
11:30 am – 2:30 pm

Monday – Thursday
4:30 pm – 10 pm

Friday
4:30 pm – 10:30 pm

Saturday
11:30 am – 10:30 pm

Sunday
11:30 am – 10 pm

**Reservations**
Recommended

**Cards**
V, MC, Debit

**Drinks**
Full bar
Corkage $10/bottle

**Outdoor Dining**
None

**Noise**
◁ – ◀)

**Price Range**
$ – $$

**Website**
szechuanrestaurant.ca

# Taste

TASTE, on the 1st Street side of Hotel Arts, is tiny—as in about 30 seats, an open kitchen that fits two cooks in close quarters and a short bar. There's little storage, no freezer, not a lot of room for much of anything. Most restaurateurs would ignore this space because of its size.

But Taste's owners think differently. They've developed a short, frequently shifting, cross-cultural dinner menu of small plates like beef tartare, perogies, kimchi asparagus, beet gnocchi, and what they call "pig wings," a tasty pork rib dish. Lunch is less oriented to the tapas style with choices like a Niçoise salad and a chicken-pesto sandwich.

The wine list is equally compact and smart. There are six reds and six whites. Period. They change every month and follow specific themes such as Italian reds paired with California whites. Taste also pours cocktails, unique beers and brown liquor: bourbon, rye, Scotch and rum.

We chose four small plates at dinner for the two of us, each ranging from $7 to $13. There were charcuterie and cheese boards at $22, but we didn't go there. Following a tapas approach, the dishes come out when the dishes come out. So our green beans coated in a Sriracha chili sauce with garlic and sesame seeds arrived first. Lively, brightly spiced beans. The prawn tacos—sliced, chilled prawns rolled up with cabbage in small flour tortillas dressed with salsa—were next. Then chicken in waffles, one of those odd food combos that actually works, followed by good cheese perogies with sausage gravy.

Taste may be small in size, but it's big in flavour.

## Address
1210 – 1 Street SW
(East side of Hotel Arts)

## Phone
403.233.7730

## Hours
Monday & Tuesday
11:30 am – 2 pm
4 pm – 11 pm

Wednesday & Thursday
11:30 am – 11 pm

Friday & Saturday
11:30 am – midnight

Sunday
4 pm – 10 pm

## Reservations
Not accepted

## Cards
V, MC, Debit

## Drinks
Full bar
No corkage

## Outdoor Dining
Small patio

## Noise
◁) – ◁))

## Price Range
$ – $$

## Website
taste-restaurant.com

# Teatro

Modern Italian

**W**HEN Teatro splashed onto the Calgary dining scene in 1993, it immediately became THE hot spot in downtown, occupying the historic Dominion Bank building (a century old in 2011) and serving stylish Italian cuisine. We loved the high ceilings, the open kitchen with the wood-fired oven and the sleek bar along one side.

And Teatro has matured into one of the city's finest eateries. Much of that can be credited to a long list of excellent chefs who have helmed Teatro's seasonal kitchen, talents like Michael Allemeier and Dominique Moussu. The latest in that line is executive chef John Michael MacNeil, a creative lad from Cape Breton. Whether it's Italian classics such as prawn chitarra (long pasta sliced with a harp-like cutter) in a lobster bisque ($28) or contemporary dishes such as the smoothest, creamiest chocolate ice cream we've ever had (frozen with liquid nitrogen), he brings style and substance to the plate. His eight-course tasting menu ($135 per person) is a decadent way to spend an evening. Even a lunch burger ($21) of ground strip loin with Appenzeller cheese, caramelized onion and bacon (plus frites) is sublime.

Along the way, there have been changes. The wood-fired oven is gone, replaced by a gleaming rotisserie that spins out a variety of tasty meats. (A beautiful aroma goes along with it.) At the same time, they introduced softer seating and stylish sound baffling, too.

But luckily, one thing has never changed. The seafood lasagna ($39) is still on the menu and is still a popular seller. Not cheap, but good to know the classics are honoured here.

**Address**
200 Stephen Avenue SE
(Olympic Plaza)

**Phone**
403.290.1012

**Hours**
Monday – Friday
11:30 am – close

Saturday & Sunday
5 pm – close

**Reservations**
Accepted

**Cards**
V, MC, AE, Debit

**Drinks**
Full bar
Corkage $35/bottle

**Outdoor Dining**
Patio

**Noise**
◁) – ◁))

**Price Range**
$$$ – $$$$

**Website**
teatro.ca

downtown calgary

# Thai Bistro

Hidden amid the warren of buildings in Chinatown are a few decidedly non-Chinese restaurants. Some are Vietnamese, a few are Japanese and one is Thai. That's Thai Bistro. Since 2008, it's brightened a dowdy address on Centre Street and proved popular enough that, in 2012, the owners opened a second location. This one, on 17th Avenue just west of 14th Street SW, has the bonus of good parking in the back.

Thai Bistro serves Central Thai cuisine. That's a style that emphasizes the fragrant flavours of Thai basil, ginger and lime over the creaminess of coconut milk or the heat of chilies. It has layers of flavour and depth throughout, with an overall soothing tone. It doesn't present a slap-you-in-the-face kind of heat like some Thai styles; it's a kinder, gentler version suitable for those who think Thai food is too spicy. The food here can still tingle your tonsils, but the chefs first build a base of flavour.

Both locations serve the same menu of kanom jeen (room-temperature noodles with your choice of red or green curry chicken, beef, pork or seafood), khao ob sapparod (fried rice with cashews, egg, pineapple, and curry, again topped with your choice of protein) and larb salad (room-temp shallots, cilantro, onion, plus a protein). The mango salad tossed with peppers, shallots, fresh chilies, dried shrimp and peanuts is particularly mouth-puckering and tangy. Thai Bistro has a long menu—83 items— which is then multiplied by all those protein choices.

And enhanced by gracious service, another marker of a good Thai restaurant.

**Address**
102, 233 Centre Street S

**Phone**
587.887.7373

**Hours**
Monday – Friday
11:30 am – 2 pm

Daily
5 pm – 9:30 pm

 downtown
calgary

---

**Address**
1448 – 17 Avenue SW

**Phone**
587.887.7474

**Hours**
Monday – Friday
11:30 am – 2 pm
5 pm – 10 pm

Saturday & Sunday
1 pm – 10 pm

---

**Common Info**

**Reservations**
Recommended

**Cards**
V, MC, Debit

**Drinks**
Full bar
Corkage $12/bottle

**Outdoor Dining**
None

**Noise**
◁ – ◁»

**Price Range**
$$

**Website**
thaibistro.ca

# Thai Boat

Thai

**T**ROLLING the area around Barlow Trail and 32nd Avenue NE for a good meal can be tricky. There are some fine independent restaurants nearby, but this is largely chain territory. One light that shines brightly amid the din of chains is that of Thai Boat. (I mean that literally, too, as their blue neon sign is both bright and attractive.)

Thai Boat has a bit of a beach and nautical theme. Booths are surrounded by bamboo curtains, replicating a beach bar, and the bar itself is shaped like a boat. Plateware is light green and adorned with a ring of elephants, and pounded tin pots are filled with rice (coconut, optional). It's a pleasant surrounding, especially considering it was once a strip-mall bank.

Thai Boat's menu covers a lot of territory and is one of the most eclectic of local Thai lists. Seriously. Numerous fonts have been used in printing it, too, and sections of it hive-off into "specials" and "kitchen feasts" and various dinners for groups. A far cry from the typically well-organized Thai menu, it still works though.

And there are some gems on it. The yum nua angun and the Crying Tiger are both beef dishes delightfully sharp with chilies and lime. The Muay Thai seafood dish is packed with lively flavours from the deep, and the "drunken" seafood is boozy, basil infused and chili hot. For those who like it milder, the pad see-you noodles stir-fried in a dark soy sauce are rich and flavourful but devoid of heat.

Thai Boat is one of a kind—and thankfully helping break the chain of chains in the northeast.

**Address**
108, 2323 – 32 Avenue NE

**Phone**
403.291.9887

**Hours**
Monday – Friday
11 am – 2:30 pm

Monday – Saturday
5 pm – 10 pm

Sunday
5 pm – 9 pm

**Reservations**
Accepted

**Cards**
V, MC, Debit

**Drinks**
Full bar
Corkage $12/bottle

**Outdoor Dining**
None

**Noise**
◁ – ◁»

**Price Range**
$ – $$$

**Website**
No

# Thai Nongkhai

Thai

**E**ARLY every December, we have a family tree-trimming event at our house. Catherine's gang assembles en masse, the decorations are divvied up and the tree is decked out in minutes. One of the youngest members of the family is hoisted up to crown the tree with an angel (thank heavens Maddock and Wyatt have arrived recently to do this task—the next youngest, Kevin, is now 25 and getting a bit unwieldy for my shoulders).

We used to try to feed this wrecking crew after the proceedings, but the devastation wreaked on our kitchen eventually convinced us to book a long table at Thai Nongkhai instead. They're always ready for us with booster seats and chilled wine and a long list of Thai dishes. We order a swack of them, some hot, some cool to satisfy all palates, some meaty, some seafoody, some vegetarian to answer all dietary needs, and then we just dive in.

The Nongkhai team rolls everything out smoothly: the deep-fried shrimp made to look like little birds, then the som tam papaya salad followed by drunken shrimp with chili paste, panang beef curry, caramel chicken and more, until we all push back from the table declaring we won't eat again until Christmas dinner. (We lie.)

A few minutes later, Thai crepes appear, rolled around condensed milk and fried to crispiness. We groan, but they somehow disappear. Sometime later, before we slip into Thai food snoozes, we fall into the December night, plans now made for the upcoming weeks.

Just another family event elevated by an evening at Thai Nongkhai. Good for other events and dinners, too!

**Address**
10, 7400 Macleod Trail S

**Phone**
403.705.3329

**Hours**
Tuesday – Friday
11:30 am – 2 pm

Tuesday – Thursday
5 pm – 9:30 pm

Friday & Saturday
5 pm – 10:30 pm

Sunday
5 pm – 9 pm

**Reservations**
Recommended,
especially weekends

**Cards**
V, MC, Debit

**Drinks**
Full bar
Corkage $12/bottle

**Outdoor Dining**
None

**Noise**
◁))

**Price Range**
$$

**Website**
thai-nk.com

# Thai Onzon

Thai
(Vegan & Vegetarian)

**S**ISTERS Pat Chirakorn and Sonthaya Chanhao cooked wonderful Thai dishes at their family's Thai Sa-on and Thai Boat restaurants for years. But they always longed to cook the vegetarian and vegan style they ate and liked best. So they decided to open their own place and landed on a property in Cochrane.

They erected a new building on the property (the restaurant is on the main floor and their residence is upstairs) and, in the fall of 2012, opened a 40-seat vegetarian and vegan Thai restaurant. Thai Onzon ("onzon," by the way, means awesome) now offers some of the best Thai food for miles around.

To be clear, there is no meat, no seafood, no gluten, minimal egg and dairy, and no alcohol at Thai Onzon. The cuisine keys on the lively chili and lime flavours and rich curries prevalent in Thai food. Take, for example, the mango salad with chunks of ripe mango drenched in a sparkling chili-lime dressing. Or the tom kha soup spiked with lemon grass, galangal and kaffir lime leaves and smoothed by coconut milk. Or the drunken stir-fried noodles. Divine.

Thai Onzon uses some soy protein replacements and crafts "calamari" from potato starch and bread crumbs, but largely sticks with real vegetable options. Some egg and dairy are used, but can be easily deleted from dishes if so desired. And the spice level can be adjusted to your preference, so if you want more or less heat, just ask.

Hot or cool, you may become a quick convert to this unique, dare I say, "onzon" cuisine.

**Address**
115 – 5 Avenue W
Cochrane

**Phone**
403.981.1499

**Hours**
Tuesday – Saturday
11 am – 2 pm
5 pm – 9 pm

**Reservations**
Recommended

**Cards**
V, MC, Debit

**Drinks**
No alcoholic beverages

**Outdoor Dining**
Small patio

**Noise**
🔊

**Price Range**
$$ – $$$

**Website**
thai-onzonveggie.com

# Thai Sa-on

## Royal Thai

Want a crisp Sauvignon Blanc with your pad Thai, or a rich Napa Cabernet Sauvignon with your red curry beef? What's that, you say? Not your typical food and beverage combos? Well they just might be, at least at Thai Sa-on.

It has one of the best (and best priced) wine lists in the city. And that's not just considering Thai or Asian restaurants. Thai Sa-on has one of the best wine lists of any kind of restaurant in town. Owner Sam Chanhao likes a sip or two, and he's built a collection of big names, cult wines and hard-to-find gems. Be careful with your pairings though—I find the big reds duke it out with any heavily chilied dish.

Regardless of your beverage choice, Thai Sa-on continues to be a classic. The food menu is as long and complex as the wine list with its collection of Royal Thai dishes, otherwise known as "palace cuisine," and its more everyday Thai items.

I'm partial to the Thai salads here, the yum nua of beef and the yum talay of seafood, both laced with a hot dressing (not for the timid). The swimming Rama shrimp in a creamy coconut curry with peanuts and spinach is always a winner. (It's medium spicy.) And the panang kai of chicken with green peppers and basil in a different coconut curry always leaves us wanting more. (I'd order all of the above with a crisp Riesling, Pinot Grigio or Sauvignon Blanc.)

You'll enjoy the setting, too. Thai Sa-on has a beachy tone that fits perfectly with the food. And that wine.

**Address**
351–10 Avenue SW

**Phone**
403.264.3526

**Hours**
Monday – Friday
11:30 am – 2 pm

Monday – Thursday
5 pm – 10 pm

Friday & Saturday
5 pm – 11 pm

**Reservations**
Recommended

**Cards**
V, MC, AE, Debit

**Drinks**
Full bar
Corkage $15/bottle

**Outdoor Dining**
None

**Noise**
◁))

**Price Range**
$$ – $$$

**Website**
thai-sa-on.com

**downtown calgary**

# Three Ravens

**T**HERE's Rundle, Norquay, Tunnel, Sulphur and the whole Bourgeau Range. Sitting atop the Sally Borden building at the Banff Centre, my attention is drawn away from the food of Three Ravens to those spectacular mountain peaks outside. They all shine in the late-day light under impossibly blue skies. And then there's Cascade. In my mind, Cascade is how a mountain should look: tall, massive, symmetrical, imposing. That's a mountain. It's also one of the images used to promote the Banff Centre.

But back to the food and Three Ravens at the aforementioned centre.

Three Ravens shares the glassed-in top floor with Vistas, the main cafeteria of the Banff Centre. It's an elegantly simple, 60-seat room that features contemporary Canadian cuisine with dishes such as Dungeness crab layered with hearts of palm, cucumber, micro greens (grown on-site) and watermelon consommé ($18). Or honey- and ginger-glazed duck breast with black rice, amaranth and quinoa hash, pecan crumble, cranberry jam and rye whisky jus ($39). It is very good food, well served by a vested crew.

And it's pricey. The bison strip loin and braised rib is $40. The lamb rack with spinach spaetzle is $42. Even the Caesar salad is $17. Now, that does include quail eggs, shaved Sylvan Star Gouda, an olive tapenade and a truffle-infused dressing, but those numbers can creep up. Oddly, the wine prices are the opposite, with many good bottles available in the low $30s. So your bill may come out looking not so bad after all.

And then there are those mountains. How much are they worth?

**Address**
107 Tunnel Mountain Drive
(The Banff Centre)
Banff

**Phone**
403.762.6300

**Hours**
Daily
5 pm – 9 pm

**Reservations**
Recommended prior
to performances

**Cards**
V, MC, AE, Debit

**Drinks**
Full bar
No corkage

**Outdoor Dining**
None

**Noise**
◁ – ◁))

**Price Range**
$$$ – $$$$

**Website**
banffcentre.ca

# Trib | Steakhouse

**T**HE 1892-built Tribune Block housed one of Calgary's first newspapers, the one that eventually became the *Albertan* and then the *Calgary Sun*. There's a sense of history in this building, enhanced by the rustic sandstone and wood tone. That's thanks to the CA Restaurant Group who, a few years ago, took the space back to its sandstone bones, redeveloping it with a dining room downstairs and a lounge on the main floor. Smart.

While I like the cozy cruise-ship feel of the windowless dining room, I most like sitting at or near the big bar in the lounge. Here, you're surrounded by padded leather, burnished wood, smart barkeeps and more of that sandstone. It seems somehow refined.

Trib takes what they call a "backward glance to a more elegant place and time" with their food. The menu features roasts such as chateaubriand prepared with Reserve Angus beef ($84 for two or more) and Brome Lake duck à la presse, in true Normandy style ($78 for two or more). There's bacon-wrapped beef tenderloin, pork tenderloin with pork belly, and honey-roasted salmon. If you have a lust for big, meaty food, Trib is the place.

A personal favourite is the New York steak sandwich served with café de Paris butter, a roasted red pepper and tomato chutney, and grilled baguette. It's just enough to satisfy my carnivorous urges without putting me into a meat coma for the rest of the day. And somehow, the steak-and-sandstone combo seems appropriate for the space and a true taste of Calgary.

**Address**
118 Stephen Avenue SW

**Phone**
403.269.3160

**Hours**
Monday – Wednesday
11 am – 11 pm

Thursday & Friday
11 am – midnight

Saturday
4 pm – midnight

**Reservations**
Recommended

**Cards**
V, MC, AE, Debit

**Drinks**
Full bar
Corkage $25/bottle

**Outdoor Dining**
Patio

**Noise**
🔊

**Price Range**
$$$ – $$$$

**Website**
tribsteakhouse.ca

downtown calgary

# The Trough

International

**T**HE Trough is not the most obvious restaurant in Canmore. Tucked into what used to be a house, it's off the main roads where most of the restaurants reside. And being an old house, it's small, seating about 40 in two sections. It looks like one of those quiet, out-of-the-way gems we like to discover when travelling.

A word of warning though: make a reservation. A lot of others have already discovered the Trough and made it their favourite restaurant in Canmore.

Run by the Fuller family, recent arrivals from Wales, the Trough is one of the cleanest, sharpest, most tightly run restaurants in the Bow Valley. Done in shades of brown, with a short bar along one side and an open kitchen at the back, the space has been used to maximum effect. Smiling, vested servers glide about, and there's a gentle buzz to the room.

Much of that buzz is about the food, an international collection using local-first ingredients. The rack of lamb (from Fort Macleod) is rosemary crusted and comes with whipped Yukon Gold potatoes. A simple preparation, but a must-have for many. The Caesar salad is served as long, individual leaves of tender romaine hearts, each leaf filled with grilled Valbella bacon, paprika croutons, Parmesan, preserved Meyer lemon and dressing, green with basil and mint. (You eat them by hand, like a taco.) The fish nachos (salmon ceviche with toasted coconut on crispy won tons) and the Salt Spring mussels (with a coconut green curry) are excellent, too, perfectly prepared and meticulously presented.

The Trough offers up the complete package. It's one of the best.

**Address**
725 Walk of Champions
(9 Street)
Canmore

**Phone**
403.678.2820

**Hours**
Tuesday – Sunday
5:30 pm – close

**Reservations**
Recommended

**Cards**
V, MC, Debit

**Drinks**
Full bar
Corkage $30/bottle

**Outdoor Dining**
Patio

**Noise**
🔊 – 🔊

**Price Range**
$$$ – $$$$

**Website**
thetrough.ca

# Una | California-Style Pizza

ɪ ꜰ you like high-energy, loud, crowded places with great food, Una is for you. If you can get in, that is. Every square centimetre has been used to shoehorn in the maximum number of people, but there seems to be at least that many more who want to join the crowd. And since they don't take reservations, Una often has a lineup. Their door policy says they'll take your cell number and call when there's a table, and they do tweet frequently about the wait time. That helps a little, but still, you'll likely have to wait.

Most folks go for the pizza: One size, thin crust, with toppings like mushrooms, smoked mozzarella, Grana Padano and truffle oil; or bacon, smoked mozzarella, pineapple and jalapeno oil; or chorizo, roasted peppers, chickpeas and sun-dried olives. Creative stuff. Top-notch ingredients and prep. Crowded room. (Did I mention Una is loud?)

On Una's "not pizza" side, they serve salads, veal-pork meatballs, flatiron steaks, roasted broccoli with walnut vinaigrette and such. It's a Western Mediterranean-ish collection of dishes. Again, nicely prepared.

Count yourself among the lucky if you can snag a table out front. (Well, maybe not the one by the lineup.) We like the seats at the bar in front of the pizza oven. There's one booth further in the back that can handle six or so people—we've never gotten it, but we live in hope.

Regardless, grab any seat you can, order up and enjoy. Una always energizes us with its combo of pizza, wine, people and noise. This is one place where it all manages to work together.

**Address**
618 – 17 Avenue SW

**Phone**
403.453.1183

**Hours**
Daily
11:30 am – 1 am

**Reservations**
Not accepted

**Cards**
V, MC, AE, Debit

**Drinks**
Full bar
No corkage

**Outdoor Dining**
Small patio

**Noise**
🔊

**Price Range**
$$

**Website**
unapizzeria.com

# Vero | Mediterranean Fusion

I HAVE a weakness for eggs Benedict. If I see it on a menu—unless there's something else pretty spectacular—odds are I'm going to order it. I've had some beauties over the years, ones where the traditional ham has been replaced with seared tuna or duck breast or even a slab of home-grown beef tenderloin.

So my biggest conundrum with brunch at Vero Bistro Moderne is which of the three distinct Benedicts to order, none of them being traditional. There's a Montreal smoked meat Benny with local Brassica mustard, arugula and wild boar bacon. Sound good? Then there's a vegetarian option of roasted organic shiitake mushrooms with sautéed kale. Nice. But there's also one with smoked salmon, a couple of jumbo prawns and arugula. All are done with poached eggs, of course, and are on house-baked phyllo pastry and draped with hand-whipped hollandaise.

For me, it's the salmon and prawn version. It's great, with layers of texture and clear, sharp flavours—perfect for waking up those weekend morning taste buds.

If you happen into Vero at other times of the day, you'll find a tasty collection of Mediterranean-inspired, globally influenced dishes such as hand-rolled sweet potato gnocchi with maple syrup, wild boar bacon, walnuts and Gorgonzola (sounds like it could be for breakfast, lunch or dinner) or steamed, wild-caught sea bass with lemon risotto.

This is beautifully prepared food by chef/owner Jenny Chan and her team, many of whom have been with her since she opened in 2008. And worthy of many a visit, even if just for the Bennies.

**Address**
209 – 10 Street NW

**Phone**
403.283.8988

**Hours**
Tuesday – Friday
11:30 am – 2 pm

Saturday & Sunday
9:30 am – 3 pm

Tuesday – Sunday
5 pm – close

**Reservations**
Recommended,
especially weekends

**Cards**
V, MC, Debit

**Drinks**
Full bar
No corkage

**Outdoor Dining**
Patio

**Noise**
🔊

**Price Range**
$$ – $$$$

**Website**
verobistro.ca

# Vin Room

**B**EWARE the plethora of choices at Vin Room if you're one of those who has a hard time deciding which wine to have with your meal, though I'm betting you can handle it.

The two Vin Rooms each have a battery of Enomatic wine dispensers that allows them to offer 64 wines by the glass. Add in a dozen sparkling wines and a dozen sweet ones, and you have a mind-boggling selection of vino from which to choose, all available as two- or six-ounce pours or as half or full bottles. That's not even counting more that's available only by the bottle. So, whatever you want will be close at hand, from a simple Chardonnay or Merlot to a much more esoteric choice. If you're into exploring wine, this is the place.

Vin Room sets up a dinner menu of tapas that's identical at both locations. It ranges from a bone marrow soufflé and chickpea fritters to grilled prawns in a sake-ginger-basil broth and lobster nachos. The lunch menu carries some of the same tapas, plus heartier stuff like burgers, penne carbonara and a daily sandwich special. Dessert includes uptempo s'mores and a silky lemon-thyme-white chocolate tart with blueberry compote.

In spite of the wine and food similarities, the two Vin Rooms each have their own character. The Mission location is squeezed into a century-old building, is louder and has a great deck. The basement and main floor were damaged in the 2013 flood, but they made a quick comeback. The new West Springs spot is high-ceilinged and airy, with roomy dining and a large bar.

Either place, you won't go hungry...or thirsty.

**Address**
2310 – 4 Street SW

**Phone**
403.457.5522

**Hours**
Sunday & Monday
4 pm – close

Tuesday – Saturday
11:30 am – close

---

**Address**
3102, 8561 – 8A Avenue SW

**Phone**
587.353.8812

**Hours**
Sunday & Monday
3 pm – 11 pm

Tuesday – Saturday
11 am – close

---

**Common Info**

**Reservations**
Recommended

**Cards**
V, MC, AE, Debit

**Drinks**
Full bar
No corkage

**Outdoor Dining**
Patios

**Noise**
◁) – ◁))

**Price Range**
$$ – $$$

**Website**
vinroom.com

# Wa's
## Japanese

Here's one for the sushi nerds, those aficionados who only accept hand-rolled sushi cakes, expertly cut fish and crisp nori (none of that soggy grocery-store stuff), those who go out of their way to find the most obscure, hole-in-the-wall joints serving the best. Wa's is for them.

Wa's is a tiny spot north of 16th Avenue along Centre Street N. It's recessed from the street with a small—and incredibly difficult to negotiate—parking lot out front. It's not new; it's been there for years, churning out great sushi in near solemnity. While some sushi bars are lively and loud, Wa's is almost monastic. You feel you have to speak in hushed tones so as not to interfere with the relationship between customers and their next piece of nigiri or maki.

Each cut of fish is precise, each piece, immaculate. Creativity creeps in with the likes of the Sunrise roll of smoked salmon, fresh salmon, avocado, cream cheese and sliced lemon. Artfully classic presentation shows up on their chirashi platters, with sashimi meticulously arranged over large bowls of sushi rice. Wa's rice, some of the lightest, perfectly sweet grains in the city, pulls all the sushi together. It is very good.

Wa's also has a full list of donburis, tempuras, ramen and such. An amazing range and depth of dishes comes out of this tiny kitchen. There's no flash, no special effects—each dish is delivered with respect. Which is just the way the sushi nerds want it.

But if you're one of those brethren, you already knew this, didn't you?

**Address**
1721 Centre Street N

**Phone**
403.277.2077

**Hours**
Tuesday – Saturday
11:30 am – 2 pm
5 pm – close

**Reservations**
Accepted

**Cards**
V, MC, AE, Debit

**Drinks**
Full bar
No corkage

**Outdoor Dining**
None

**Noise**
◁

**Price Range**
$$

**Website**
wascalgary.exblog.jp

# Wellington's | Steakhouse, Fine Dining

**O**LD school.
    Linens on the table. Seafood Newburg on the menu, black vests on the staff. Service that's about the customer, not the server. That's Wellington's. When I say old school, I mean it in a very good way.

Many of the older, classic restaurants have become tired or have disappeared. Wellington's is still here after almost 35 years, and they've stay around by serving expertly prepared food, refreshing their look frequently and honing their service skills to a knife's edge. Even the bus boy, a deft hand with the ice water and bacon bits, impressed us. As for the servers themselves, they are capital *P* Professionals: there when they should be, friendly enough but not in search of a new best friend. Appropriate for one of Calgary's finest steakhouses.

Wellington's serves a breadth of Calgarians: suited lunchers, gussied-up daters, whole families out for a good meal. They all have one thing in common—a carnivorous lust for Wellington's beef and other classic steakhouse fare. Like the shrimp cocktails of huge, crunchy crustaceans served, with piquant sauce, in the silver and crystal plateware built for such things. And the Caesar salad, made tableside and plated in huge mounds of beautiful, lemony, garlicky, Tabasco-y, anchovy splendor.

And those steaks. Sterling Silver (the top end of AAA) rib-eyes and tenderloins, perfectly seasoned and grilled in clear view through a Plexiglas booth. Great beef, served up with mushrooms, baked or stuffed potatoes, and no unnecessary greens.

And to finish? Tableside-flamed cherries jubilee—a classic for a reason. Like I said, old school. In a good way.

**Address**
10325 Bonaventure Drive SE

**Phone**
403.278.5250

**Hours**
Monday – Friday
11:30 am – 1:30 pm

Monday – Saturday
5:30 pm – close

Sunday
4:30 pm – 8:30 pm

**Reservations**
Recommended

**Cards**
V, MC, AE, Debit

**Drinks**
Full bar
No corkage

**Outdoor Dining**
None

**Noise**
◁ – ◁)

**Price Range**
$$ – $$$$

**Website**
wellingtonsofcalgary.com

# White Elephant | Thai

**I**F you find White Elephant on your first try, consider yourself lucky. It's in the Pointe Inn behind the Radisson hotel, just north of 16th Avenue and east of Deerfoot. (I'm hoping that'll give you a hand locating it.) White Elephant leases a couple of rooms there and has installed a 60-seat Thai restaurant, which includes a colourful mural of the owners' family farm in Thailand.

Now to the name. In Thailand, a white elephant is a symbol of justice, power and prosperity. The Thai government even inducts those whose deeds they deem worthy into the Most Exalted Order of the White Elephant. In Western culture, we think of white elephants in a much different way, usually as a costly, unwieldy venture.

Fortunately, this White Elephant leans to the Thai side of things. The food here tastes more like what I've tried in Thailand than any place I've been this side of the Pacific. (And frankly, it's better than a lot I've had in Thailand because meats are so much better here.) White Elephant brings in fresh herbs, spices, seafood and vegetables weekly from Thailand, some of which are from their farm there, and they prepare them all with skill and a smile. It's a family-run operation where each and every dish is handcrafted to order.

It's hard to say what to try here. The menu is long and diverse, with a lovely blend of hot and mild dishes. Everything I've had, I've liked. (And I've had a lot.) So go with your own preferences or just close your eyes and point to something. White Elephant will provide.

**Address**
1808 – 19 Street NE
(The Pointe Inn)

**Phone**
403.457.1172

**Hours**
Tuesday, Thursday & Friday
11:30 am – 1 pm

Monday – Saturday
5 pm – 9 pm

**Reservations**
Recommended

**Cards**
V, MC, AE, Debit

**Drinks**
Full bar
No corkage

**Outdoor Dining**
None

**Noise**
◁))

**Price Range**
$$

**Website**
whiteelephantcuisine
calgary.com

# Without Papers

I F you like your pizza parlour up a steep set of stairs in a lively, loud room with black and white movies playing on the walls and a cheeky attitude (check out the name), then Without Papers might be your place. Without Papers is fun. And, by the way, the pizza is pretty darn good, too (and you can also get it from their cheeky food truck—the one with "Pizza Emergency" plastered across the front).

Angelo Contrada and Jesse Johnson have created a Neapolitan-style pizzeria that blends a bit of the Old World with the New. Contrada tosses, then tops his margherita pizza with a simple but rich tomato sauce, fresh basil and fior di latte mozzarella (made in the traditional Bojano style at White Gold in northeast Calgary) and lays it on the rotating stone floor of his huge custom-made oven. Then he'll top another pizza, maybe this one with wild boar sausage, braised rapini and fontina cheese, and a third, perhaps with spicy cacciatore salami, Calabrese salami, peperonata and more mozzarella. The robustly flavoured combos are always changing, and seemingly anything goes. The Hawaii 5-o includes back bacon, pineapple, cheddar and jalapenos, and it's great.

Beyond pizza, Without Papers serves calzone and a nice list of salads, including a roasted vegetable-quinoa one and another of roasted beets and goat feta. On the sweet side, you can get a black cherry cola or even a banana split. But my choice for dessert has to be the Sweet Julie pizza topped with ricotta, banana and Nutella.

As they say, when in Naples…

## Address
1216 – 9 Avenue SE
(Second Floor)

## Phone
403.457.1154

## Hours
Monday – Saturday
11 am – 10 pm

Sunday
4 pm – 9 pm

## Reservations
Recommended

## Cards
V, MC, AE, Debit

## Drinks
Beer & wine
No corkage

## Outdoor Dining
None

## Noise
◁))

## Price Range
$$

## Website
wopizza.ca

# Xocolat

**F**IRST things first. The name is pronounced "shuck-o-lat," derived from the Nahuatl (language of the Aztecs) words for bitter (xococ) and water (atl). It describes how chocolate was first consumed as a bitter liquid made from a paste of pounded cocoa beans. But there's nothing bitter about Xocolat, the posh Mexican restaurant that took over the former Virginia Christopher Gallery.

So what is posh Mexican? Well, there's the setting. Not a sombrero or piece of folk art in the place. Instead, there's a copper-toned epoxy floor, an onyx bar with complementing hanging onyx lights, volcanic cantera stone tiles on the walls and an open kitchen at one end. Truckloads of wood tables and padded chairs were shipped in from Mexico to give the place a very upscale, contemporary look.

The menu follows suit. It's Mexican, but contemporary Mexican. So you'll find updated versions of Caesar salad ($14), chilaquiles ($20) and a chile relleno ($19) alongside a lamb barbacoa with chickpeas ($34) and a veal chop with Xocolat sauce and lentils ($36). The dishes are presented on the large white plates favoured by contemporary restaurants and priced accordingly. So $2 tacos wrapped in paper are not what you'll find here.

This is very good food, creatively conceived and skilfully prepared. One dessert—a tequila mousse—stands out as a showstopper. A large globe of frozen lime juice is filled with tequila mousse, providing a silky-crunchy texture and the flavour of a frozen margarita. With perhaps a shot of tequila or mescal to complete the experience, it's a fine finish to your meal.

**Address**
816 – 11 Avenue SW

**Phone**
403.264.6555

**Hours**
Monday – Friday
11 am – 3 pm

Monday – Wednesday
5 pm – 10 pm

Thursday – Saturday
5 pm – late

**Reservations**
Recommended

**Cards**
V, MC, AE, Debit

**Drinks**
Full bar
No corkage

**Outdoor Dining**
None

**Noise**
◁) – ◁))

**Price Range**
$$$ – $$$$

**Website**
xocolat.ca

# Yellow Door

## Bistro Inspired

Wᴴᴇɴ Saint Germain shuffled off to restaurant heaven, its leased space reverted to Hotel Arts, so the team there created Yellow Door (yes, it has a yellow door). At last, Hotel Arts has an all-purpose room for breakfast-lunch-dinner options.

They completed a stylish renovation, creating a hive of areas flexible enough for large functions, discreet dinners and that hotel necessity—a comfortable table for the single diner. The new room is much brighter and lighter than its predecessor. One wall is covered in antique wooden shutters from Belgium. (Why? It works.) Some of the chairs look like they were built by Lego for an adult kindergarten. (Why? It works.) A number of tables can latch together or collapse into smaller tops. (Why? You get the picture.) Throughout the black, grey and white theme, there are yellow highlights. (They work, too.)

The menu is a lovely blend of contemporary and classic. From a changing breakfast buffet (à la carte is available as well) with the likes of lemon ricotta pancakes or a duck confit cassoulet with poached eggs to dinner classics of saddle of lamb and bouillabaisse, the menu far exceeds most hotel dining rooms. The Dungeness crab salad is a texture- and flavour-filled treat of sliced apple, charred grapefruit, lettuce and copious amounts of fresh crab in a coconut-citrus vinaigrette. The serrano flatbread with Espelette peppers, Taleggio cheese and cantaloupe is refreshing and filling at the same time.

There's great variety here, helping Hotel Arts meet the needs of all their clients, whether they're hotel visitors or Calgarians looking for a good meal.

**Address**
119 – 12 Avenue SW
(Hotel Arts)

**Phone**
403.206.9585

**Hours**
Daily
6:30 am – 11 pm

**Reservations**
Accepted

**Cards**
V, MC, AE, Debit

**Drinks**
Full bar
No corkage

**Outdoor Dining**
None

**Noise**
◁ – ◁»)

**Price Range**
$$ – $$$

**Website**
yellowdoorbistro.ca

# Zipang

I CAN'T be the only person who typically doesn't like miso soup. The obligatory start to many Japanese meals, I so often find it to be dishwatery, limp and even grainy if the tofu breaks down. There'll often be some flaccid nori in it—its only purpose seemingly to get stuck in your teeth. Blecch!

Then I go to Zipang and I realize that miso soup can be deep with flavour, the broth lively, the tofu creamy, the nori lush. Why can't everyone make it like this? The miso here shows Zipang's commitment and attention to quality.

They also have the full menu of tempura, noodles, donburis and such, and one of these days I'm going to try them, but I never seem to get past the sushi. With a bowl of miso, of course.

The sushi cuts are thick and exact—I've never had to dance around a long filament in the fish. These are among the most precise cuts in the city. And the rice—it's always perfect. I like that the assorted sushi lunch ($16.50) comes with a choice of salad or a bowl of that sushi rice. Plus the miso. And the rice here at Zipang is worth an extra bowl. Especially with a dousing of low-salt soy sauce and some fresh wasabi. (Zipang carries real wasabi, as well as the more common green-coloured product, and they often have more unique sushi choices than other places, choices such as tuna belly or spot prawns.)

And did I mention that miso? Another bowl of that too, please.

**Address**
1010 – 1 Avenue NE

**Phone**
403.262.1888

**Hours**
Monday – Friday
11:30 am – 2 pm

Monday – Saturday
5 pm – 9 pm

**Reservations**
Recommended

**Cards**
V, MC, AE, JCB, Debit

**Drinks**
Full bar
Corkage $5/person

**Outdoor Dining**
None

**Noise**
🔊

**Price Range**
$$ – $$$

**Website**
zipang.ca

## Barpa Bill's

Greek Fast Food

223 Bear Street
Banff
403.762.0377

**T**HE garlicky tang of Barpa Bill's lamb souvlaki—packed with spices and rolled with tomatoes, tzatziki and greens into a soft pita—is right off an Athens street corner. Even the Barpa Burger has a garlicky bite to it. (Bill goes through 10 pounds of fresh garlic each week.) Enjoy the casual tone and be careful who you breathe on.

## The Better Butcher

Meat Market

377 Heritage Drive SE
(Acadia Centre)
403.252.7171

**A**RMED with a sharp knife and an encyclopedic knowledge of meat, Randy Hnatuk carves some of the best meat in the city. It's always locally raised, perfectly aged and precisely trimmed to maximize flavour and tenderness. And if you're looking for that hard-to-find ingredient (duck fat, anyone?) or special cut (flatiron steaks?), this is the place. There's some fresh produce, too.

**downtown calgary**

## Black Betty

Burger & Wine Bar

606 – 1 Street SW
403.265.4230

blackbettybwb.com

**B**URGERS, burgers and more burgers are on offer at Black Betty in the historic Lougheed Building. Ground chuck (or pork or Wagyu beef) is grilled and topped with lots of variation, like sauerkraut or grilled pineapple or pickled carrots or apple wood-smoked cheddar. For the non-burger fan, there's tuna tataki, barbecued pork flatbread and chicken wings by the pound.

downtown calgary

# Bliss & Co.

## Cupcake & Dessert Bakery

**T**HE cupcake craze continues unabated after more than a decade. The ones I like best come from Bliss & Co. The original Chinatown spot is now for pre-orders only, but all locations have the red velvet, vanilla, chocolate, lemon, coconut and carrot cupcakes topped with numerous flavours of icing. Add in brownies, fruit pies, macaroons and flourless cupcakes, and dessert is covered.

103 – 3 Avenue SW
(Lower Level)
403.281.8821

6455 Macleod Trail S
(Chinook Centre)
403.281.8837

205 – 5 Avenue SW
(Bow Valley Square 2)
403.699.8838

blisscupcakes.ca

# Blu

## Seafood & Market

**A**s seafood shops go, there are none better than Blu. Owner Brian Plunkett is a consummate chef who creates salmon burgers, seafood brochettes and pot pies to sell along with fresh cuts of fish and crab and lobster live from the tank (there's fresh meat, too). His shop is full of fishy accessories like oyster knives and a gazillion suggestions on how to cook seafood.

9675 Macleod Trail S
(Brick Plaza)
403.252.2330

510 –77 Avenue SE
(Calgary Farmers' Market)
No phone

blusea.ca

# Blue Door

## Oils & Vinegars

**T**HE olive oil and balsamic vinegar movement is alive and well at Blue Door with dozens of international EVOOS (plain, flavour-fused and flavour-infused) and as many balsamics, both white and dark, in flavours like Sicilian lemon, maple and espresso. Specialty oils (like roasted almond, roasted sesame, roasted walnut) and specialty vinegars (like honey, Pinot Noir, champagne) round out the fare.

3126, 8561 – 8A Avenue SW
587.353.6888

14555 Symons Valley Road NW
(Symons Valley Ranch)
No phone

bluedoorcalgary.com

## Boogie's | Burgers

Calgary's best fast-food burgers are at Boogie's. That includes the "Doug's Don't Fear the Reaper" burger of four beef patties, four slices of bacon, a wiener, two slices of cheddar, a fried egg and a mini corndog. Add a peanut butter and jam milkshake and some spicy fries and you are tempting fate, man. (But I lived to write about it. And OK, I shared it.)

908 Edmonton Trail NE
403.230.7070

boogiesburgers.com

## Braizen | Braised Meats

From their jerk chicken to their heavy-duty breakfasts, Braizen food truck offers substantial fare with abundant flavour. The Braizen gang likes to braise, as in cook low and slow for a long time, maximizing the meatiness. But the food, often formed into sliders, goes down way quicker than it took to cook. Try the chipotle pork tacos.

Food Truck
403.650.1941

## Bridgeland Market | Neighbourhood Market

Bridgeland Market used to be a funky corner grocery store, but Yousef Traya (his family owns Tazza across the street) has upscaled it with a charcuterie bar, fine cheeses, quality produce, international dry goods and a tasty pop-up ice cream bar courtesy of Fiasco Gelato. Prices remain reasonable, including the best deal on serrano ham in town. Check out the sign on the west side of the building—it's always engaging.

1104 – 1 Avenue NE
403.269.2381

## Brix and Morsel

Globally Inspired

1213 – 1 Street SW
Phone TBA

brixandmorsel.com

**G**ARTH Brown, former manager of both Olives and the Tribune, has a multi-layered, well-conceived plan to convert an old 1st Street SW brick building into a lively restaurant and lounge called Brix and Morsel. Only one problem: it was still under construction at press time. It's a huge project, but with Brown's professionalism, I expect it to be a good one (opening in fall 2013).

## Calgary Farmers' Market

Farmers' Market

510 – 77 Avenue SE
403.240.9113

calgaryfarmersmarket.ca

**W**ITH over 80 vendors—from Gull Valley Greenhouses, Spragg's Meat Shop and the Silk Road Spice Merchant to Cherry Pit, Innisfail Growers and the Main Dish—the Calgary Farmers' Market offers fresh products to cook yourself, ingredients to add to the mix and prepared foods for immediate consumption. Plus a fun, family atmosphere year-round.

## Chocolaterie Bernard Callebaut

Chocolatier

1313 – 1 Street SE
403.266.4300

bernardcallebaut.com

**C**HOCOLATERIE Bernard Callebaut—now owned by Cococo Chocolatiers—remains the classic Belgian-Calgarian chocolate shop we've known and loved for over 30 years. Step into the main showroom here to view a palate-boggling array of chocolatey options and snag a sample or two. There are a dozen or so outlets around town and in Banff (check the website for locations), a few of which include Cococo cafés serving hot chocolate and gelato.

## Clive Burger

Burgers

736 – 17 Avenue SW
403.229.9224

cliveburger.com

**U**SING naturally raised beef, quality ingredients and 100 percent compostable packaging, Clive Burger represents the next step in fast food. Burgers, smokies, fries and custard-based milkshakes (try the morello cherry one!) are what Clive does and does very well. There's a patio here and loads of seats inside. Look for more Clives to pop up around town soon.

## Clubhouse at Stewart Creek

Upscale Clubhouse

4100 Stewart Creek Drive
(Stewart Creek Golf Club)
Canmore
403.609.6099

stewartcreekgolf.com

**W**HILE crusty hot dogs do a rotisserie dance at many golf clubhouses, a few other courses, like Stewart Creek, exceed the usual vittles with smoked salmon burgers, bread bowls filled with clam chowder or chili, grilled vegetable salads with aged sherry vinegar, seared sablefish and quinoa burgers. The course is private, but the restaurant is open to all.

## Cookbook Co. Cooks

All Things Culinary

722–11 Avenue SW
403.265.6066

cookbookcooks.com

**T**HE Cookbook Co., located in the Beltline, specializes in hard-to-find ingredients (like white anchovies or French crème fraîche). They also stock cookware and have the best collection of cookbooks in the city. And check out their cooking classes, either for personal enrichment or for a fun group activity. This all-purpose food organization does catering and culinary tours, too.

**Craft Beer Market**

Modern Beer Hall

**O**VER 100 international beers are on tap at any given time at Craft (the most in Canada they say), providing a liquid backdrop to some remarkably good pub food. Miso-marinated halibut and butternut squash ravioli line up with chipotle-braised lamb and a chopped kale salad on the rich, intelligent menu—great for pairing with beer.

345 – 10 Avenue SW
403.514.2337

craftbeermarket.ca

---

**CRMR at Home**

Culinary Shop

**I**F you've enjoyed the mustard melons or the elk osso bucco on a visit to one of Canadian Rocky Mountain Resorts' restaurants, now you can take some home. That's what CRMR at Home is about—sending a little taste of the CRMR properties to your kitchen. They also hold cooking classes and offer specialty culinary products, from top-notch cutting boards to environmentally friendly cleaning products.

330 – 17 Avenue SW
403.532.0241

crmr.com

---

**Crossroads Market**

Farmers' Market

**S**INCE 1987, Crossroads Market has provided a lively outlet for farm-fresh foods and a broad—and occasionally wacky—collection of other products. Always improving, a renovation in 2013 added 28 new vendors to the farmers' market section, including Greens, Eggs & Ham, Nefiss Lezziz Olives, Pearson's Berry Farm, Broxburn Vegetables and the Flat Crepe.

1235 – 26 Avenue SE
403.291.5208

crossroadsmarket.ca

**downtown calgary**

## Decadent Desserts

### Dessert Bakery

**F**OR over three decades, Decadent Desserts has been the ultimate place to go for exquisite cakes, over-the-top tarts, and cookies and cheesecakes of all sorts. This is baking that combines style with substance. Order a cake here—the luscious coconut one, for example—and you'd better have someone with enough upper body strength to heft it around. And a ready crew to consume it.

831 – 10 Avenue SW
403.245.5535

decadentdesserts.ca

## The Eddie

### Gourmet Burgers

**B**IG-TIME, big-sized burgers are Eddie's biz, from the Classic ($14) with AAA Alberta beef, cheddar, bacon, grilled onion and pickle on an onion bun to the King Eddie ($299), one pound of Wagyu beef with any toppings you'd like and a bottle of 2005 Joseph Phelps Insignia. Either way, you won't leave the Eddie hungry.

211 Caribou Street
Banff
403.762.2230

eddieburgerbar.ca

## El Charrito

### Taqueria

**T**HE little taqueria on Edmonton Trail provides legit Jalisco-style tacos, double-wrapped in fresh corn tortillas. The shredded pork tacos are a fave here, as are the chiles rellenos. I'm even happy with the chips and salsa or guacamole while I watch Mexican soap operas and soccer on the televisions. Note: They also have a small collection of Mexican ingredients for sale.

808 Edmonton Trail NE
403.478.2924

## Epiphanie Chocolate

### Chocolatier

**D**EBRA Fleck shows a passion for fine chocolate in her exquisite, handcrafted creations. Chocolates and truffles are infused with mouth-watering flavours like top-quality vanilla, organic ginger or Earl Grey tea. They're perfect for savouring after a good meal. You can even special-order chocolates decorated with your own picture (or logo). Epiphanie chocolates are also on the dessert menu at Farm.

1417–11 Street SW
403.370.4592

epiphaniechocolate.com

---

downtown calgary

## Falafel King

### Lebanese

**T**HE room is long and narrow and sometimes the lineup is long, but the welcome at Falafel King is warm and the food, satisfying. The scent of freshly squeezed juices and spit-roasted meats fill the air (I'm partial to the OJ and the chicken shawarma), and the falafel is always hot and fresh. It's just as it should be in this tiny kingdom on Stephen Avenue.

225A Stephen Avenue SW
403.269.5464

falafelking.ca

---

## Fiasco Gelato

### Artisan Gelato

**T**HERE's no tinny music playing when the Fiasco truck pulls up. Instead, this new-age ice cream truck brings a gourmet line of frequently rotating, fresh-made treats such as burnt-sugar or cayenne-chocolate gelato and raspberry-lime or mojito sorbetto. Choose from 8 mobile flavours, 16 at their pop-up outlet in Bridgeland Market or dozens at their production shop. Look for their second truck too, Bambino by Fiasco.

416 Meridian Road SE
403.452.3150

1104 – 1 Avenue NE
(Bridgeland Market)
403.269.2381

fiascogelato.ca

## Flavours | Nigerian

**L**OOKING for suya (thinly sliced spiced beef), asun (barbecued goat), asaro (yam porridge) or a goat and pepper soup? You'll find them at Flavours, Calgary's first Nigerian restaurant. The food is, as the name suggests, deeply flavoured, and it's sometimes hot too—spiced as it can be with habanero chilies. Lunch or dinner is always interesting in this colourful northwest restaurant adorned with Nigerian mementos.

4129 – 4 Street NW
403.719.1222

flavourcuisineandcatering.com

## Gaga Pizzeria | Pizza

**S**PINACH, prosciutto, bocconcini and figs. Ham, bacon, prunes and feta. These are the kinds of pizzas you'll find at Gaga, arranged on organic-flour crusts as 8-inch personal pies or 14-inch sharing ones— those, plus fresh sandwiches, sweets, bureks (Balkan-style pastries filled with meat, cheese or potato) and a warm welcome from the owners. It's good pizza and reasonably priced, with personal ones going for $8.

1236 – 12 Avenue SW
403.264.2421

pizzeriagaga.ca

## Heartland Café | Whole Food Eatery

**A**N historic church in downtown Okotoks is the perfect backdrop for the homespun, handcrafted food of Heartland. I always enjoy the hearty soups and hefty sandwiches on house-baked bread. (You can smell the scent of fresh bread floating up from the basement kitchen.) Kick it up with meat loaf or salmon: everything is under $20 except the 10-ounce rib-eye at $28.

46 McRae Street
Okotoks
403.995.4623

heartlandcafe.ca

## Heaven | International Gluten Free

**H**EAVEN is 100 percent gluten free, it's vegan and vegetarian friendly, it's organic whenever possible and it's also very good. It has an international flare with pulled-pork arepas, Thai shrimp salad, paella and bruschetta. Mac'n'cheese fans can get their hit with quinoa pasta, and chocolate cake lovers can try a flourless version. Heaven is a simple place where the menu changes frequently under the skilled hands of chef/owner Patricia Capuzzi.

119, 1013 – 17 Avenue SW
403.249.3037

heavenartisangf.ca

 ## Holy Grill | Burgers & Paninis

**S**ANDWICHES and burgers are what Holy Grill does. (OK, plus a few sides and some eggs Benedict at breakfast.) The Gourmet Burger—all-natural beef on a whole wheat kaiser—with avocado and blue cheese is a messy, six-napkin treat, great with their sweet-potato chips. Lately they've taken to the street, too, serving prime-rib sandwiches from their SteakOut Truck (often from the parking lot at Mountain Equipment Co-op).

827 – 10 Avenue SW
403.261.9759

holygrill.ca

## Holy Smoke | Southern BBQ

**H**OLY Smoke covers the barbecue bases of pulled pork, chopped brisket and smoked chicken, each piled into thick sandwiches. They add in meaty, smoky pork ribs for a buck each. Slop on some sauce, pick up some cornbread and beans, and you're in hog heaven. And don't forget a pecan tart to finish. Now also available from their food truck.

420 – 16 Avenue NE
403.263.4659

4, 4640 Manhattan Road SE
403.605.9365

901 – 64 Avenue NE
(Food Court, Deerfoot Mall)
403.265.1185

holysmokebbq.ca

## Itza Bakeshop — Bakery

**Y**OU can smell Alexandra Chan's bakery the moment you walk into the Devenish Building. Fresh croissants, baguettes, pains au chocolat, lemon tarts and quiche are all baked daily, as are lunch treats such as cheese quiche and sausage rolls. Itza is also a destination for wedding—and other celebration—cakes. (These are wedding cakes that are actually good to eat!)

908 – 17 Avenue SW
(Devenish Building)
403.228.0044

itzabakeshop.com

---

## James Joyce — Irish Pub

**M**Y Irish friends tell me the James Joyce is more Irish than most pubs in Ireland with its high-backed wood booths, cozy snugs, long wood bar and Guinness at three temperatures. With its boxties, bangers and mash, steak and Guinness pie, chicken curry and Irish stew, the food fits too. There's even a chocolate and Guinness brownie.

114 Stephen Avenue SW
403.262.0708

jamesjoycepub.com

---

## Janice Beaton Fine Cheese — Cheese Shop

**F**OR all your cheesy comestible needs, Janice Beaton Fine Cheese answers the call with the finest artisanal cheeses available, from French Bleu des Basques to Salt Spring Island peppercorn chevre. In addition to cheese and cheese accoutrements to-go, you can have cheesy lunches of sandwiches and cheese plates at the grilled cheese bar. Or you can step next door for the full-meal deal at Farm.

1017 – 16 Avenue SW
403.229.0900

jbfinecheese.com

**downtown calgary**

## Jelly Modern | Modern Doughnuts

THE maple-bacon doughnut is divine, the Nenshi salted caramel (the mayor doesn't eat pork), decadent and the carrot cake one, enough to make any wascally wabbit smile. Fundamentally, Jelly makes a very good doughnut with very good fillings and toppings. They have redefined how we look at—and eat—the circular pastry. They also make delicious sandwiches and wedding cakes from doughnuts, and there's a truck, too.

100, 1414 – 8 Street SW
403.453.2053

510 – 77 Avenue SE
(Calgary Farmers' Market)
No phone

111 – 5 Avenue SW
(+15 Level, Suncor Energy Centre)
No phone

jellymoderndoughnuts.com

## JoJo's BBQ | Southern BBQ

THE Chariot of Smoke is always ready to serve up pulled pork and barbecued ribs under chef/driver/owner Jody Barned's learned eye. This is Southern barbecue, down and dirty from an old Chevy truck in a parking lot near you—big and smoky and messy, topped with coleslaw and mopped up with corn fritters. Warning: Don't dress for JoJo's.

Food Truck
587.896.7827

bbqcalgary.com

## The Junction | Indian & Western

DINING in Dead Man's Flats got a little more interesting with the arrival of Russell Donald and the curries and burgers he cooks up at the Junction, a small, lively place in the roadside hamlet. Butter chicken, dal masoor, hand-formed nan and chili with cornbread in the shadow of the Rockies are too good to pass by. This is the kind of pit stop we like.

120 – 1 Avenue
Dead Man's Flats
403.609.3671

thejunctionhouse.ca

## Kaffir Lime | Indonesian

**T**HE tiny Indonesian food booth in the Kingsland Farmers' Market kicks out big flavours with gado-gado, beef rendang, lemon-grass chicken, peanut-sauced satay and even satisfying rice dishes. All the fare is brightly coloured, deeply spiced and layered with textures; this is complex stuff for a food court. Look for Kaffir Lime to have its own restaurant someday soon as well as another booth at Symons Valley Ranch.

7711 Macleod Trail S
(Kingsland Farmers' Market)
403.852.7491

14555 Symons Valley Road NW
(Coming Soon)

## Kickers | Smoked Meat Deli

**T**HE small menu at Kickers Smoked Meat & Deli is almost bigger than its tiny space in the historic Radio Block. But it all revolves around Lester's smoked meat (and turkey) from Montreal, sliced into rye or sourdough and served with the requisite pickles and other accoutrements. There's smoked salmon, too. You may even be lucky enough to snag one of the 12 seats.

1215 – 1 Street SW
403.288.8860

kickersdeli.ca

## Kingsland Farmers' Market | Farmers' Market

**B**ROXBURN Vegetables, Lund's Organic Farm, Hoven Farms, Spragg's Meat Shop, Jackson's Deli, Rustic Sourdough and Field Stone Fruit Wines are just a few of the vendors found at Kingsland Farmers' Market. Parked in a former car dealership, Kingsland offers fine ingredients to take home, prepared foods to-go and tasty treats to eat on-site. There are always family friendly activities, too.

7711 Macleod Trail S
403.255.3276

kfmcalgary.com

## Knifewear | Knives

**K**NIFEWEAR answers all your knife needs, from sharpening your old dull blades to providing the niftiest, sharpest hand-forged knives from Japan. Cutting boards, shaving equipment, reading materials, Food on Your Shirt T-shirts, and sharpening and cutting classes bring it all together. New shops have opened in Kelowna and Ottawa, and pop-up shops, well, pop up frequently.

100A, 1316 – 9 Avenue SE
403.514.0577

510 – 77 Avenue SE
(Calgary Farmers' Market)
403.690.7894

knifewear.com

## Koob | Kebabs

**M**EAT on a stick is elevated to primal Persian goodness at this tiny walk-in, stand-up 4th Street boutique café they call a kebab factory. Fresh lamb, beef, chicken and vegetables are skewered and grilled over open flame and loaded into pita with a world of toppings on offer. (I like the sumac onions, corn and black bean salsa, and pomegranate sauce on the lamb kebab.)

2015 – 4 Street SW
403.926.5662

koob.ca

## La Boulangerie | Bakery Café

**T**HE plastic "wicker" chairs on the sidewalk all face to the street, just like they do in France. Inside, display cabinets are filled with lush pastries and tarts, baskets overflow with breads fresh from the oven and staff fill soup bowls and layer crepes with fruit and Nutella and other goodies. Grab a chair and enjoy the bustle of La Boulangerie.

2435 – 4 Street SW
403.984.9294

## A Ladybug | European Bakery Café

**C**OMBINING local and organic ingredients with years of Belgian baking experience, A Ladybug Bakery and Café prepares fresh and lovely cakes, pastries, crepes and so on, all available for dining in or taking home. Seasonal specials fill the display cabinets and disappear quickly, but there are always more coming out of the oven. And the bistro side of the bakery serves lovely Belgian waffles, salads and burgers. The pull a mean espresso, too.

2132, 10 Aspen Stone Boulevard SW
403.249.5530

ladybugandcafe.com

## Laggan's | Bakery Café

**N**o trip to Lake Louise is complete without a stop at Laggan's bakery café in Samson Mall. Great for pre- or post-hiking (or skiing), Laggan's always has huge piles of fresh cookies, muffins, sandwiches, pizzas and other carbo-loading goodies. The lineup is typically long, but it moves quickly and you can use the time to brush up on the myriad of languages surrounding you.

101 Village Road
(Samson Mall)
Lake Louise
403.522.2017

laggans.ca

## Las Maracas | Mexican

**B**ETWEEN the green salsa enchiladas, the guacamole and the Dos Equis beer, we felt we were back in the desert (the Linda Ronstadt music helped a bit too) instead of an Okotoks strip mall. Las Maracas makes good Mexican food, including a fine corn cake and tacos of slow-cooked pork al pastor or nicely spiced beef.

71 Riverside Drive W
(Willow Park)
Okotoks
403.995.7015

lasmaracas.ca

## L'Epicerie | French Deli

1325 – 1 Street SE
403.514.0555

lepicerieca.com

**F**OR all your French culinary needs—cheeses, pickles, charcuterie, cassoulet beans, mustards and so on—L'Epicerie makes for one-stop shopping. (I love the Comté cheese here, my favourite of the French fromages.) Founded by Dominique Moussu (now of Cassis Bistro), L'Epicerie was sold to Samuel Nedelec in 2013. He continues the French traditions and catering, and still makes wonderful madeleines and *un sandwich fantastique.*

## Lina's | Italian Market & Café

2202 Centre Street N
403.277.9166

linasmarket.com

**F**OR all your Italian kitchen needs, Lina's fits the bill. With cheeses, olives, cold cuts, fresh produce, canned goods, cookware, oils, vinegars, four kinds of risotto rice, the list goes on and on. The variety is extensive, the quality is excellent and the prices, far from the highest. It's enough to build up an appetite, which you can slake at the 40-seat café.

## Los Chilitos | Taco & Tequila House

1309 – 17 Avenue SW
403.228.5528

510 – 77 Avenue SE
(Calgary Farmers' Market)
No phone

loschilitos.ca

**L**os Chilitos, a 17th Avenue taqueria, dances with Mexican flavours and tequila drinks, especially on sunny patio days. (The split-level patio seats twice as many as the restaurant itself.) From the fish tacos and chicken fajitas to the chiles rellenos and shrimp tostadas, Los Chilitos provides a big, satisfying taste of Mexico. The Calgary Farmers' Market location serves a shorter, but no less tasty menu, sans tequila.

## Manuel Latruwe | Belgian Bakery & Café

**M**ANY sandwiches on Manuel Latruwe's multi-grain bread have fuelled this book. In addition to Latruwe's two dozen kinds of bread, there are many great pastries, croissants and cakes here, plus a freezer full of outstanding ice cream and "take and bake" products. Latruwe also serves fine breakfasts and lunches largely focused on the baking— the croque madame is terrific, but the Belgian waffles always tempt.

1333 – 1 Street SE
403.261.1092

manuellatruwe.com

## Market 17 | Gourmet Market

**P**RODUCTS from Sunworks Farm, Red Tree Catering, Tres Marias, Prairie Mill, Paradise Mountain Organic Coffee (their Angel's espresso also fuelled this book), Brassica Mustard and many, many more local purveyors fill the racks at Market 17. This is destination shopping for the food fan, complete with recipes, preparations and food suggestions. You can also pop into J. Webb Wine Merchant next door or have a bite at Vie Café inside the market.

2505 – 17 Avenue SW
(Casel Marché)
403.685.4410

market17.ca

## Menyatai | Japanese Noodles

**B**IG bowls of great ramen noodles—in broths like spicy miso, soy or curry— topped with vegetables and roast pork are served at Menyatai. The tempura, udon noodles and donburis are just as delightful. The soups are deeply flavoured and scooped with a large wooden ramen spoon, though I always ask for a smaller soup spoon. The setting is simple and colourful with the kindergarten-like plastic chairs and tables.

24 – 12 Street NW
403.263.3666

## Montagu's | Sandwiches

**K**EYING on Pret A Manger's London concept of grab-and-go sandwiches made with freshness and quality, Montagu's (named after John Montagu, the 4th Earl of Sandwich and father of the sandwich) offers quick, high-quality sandwiches on Manuel Latruwe bread. Combos like roast chicken and avocado or brie and sun-dried tomato dot the list, and great in-house baking, like the scones and banana bread, kicks it up a notch.

1306 – 1 Street SW
403.680.5830

montagus.ca

## Mug Shotz | Sports Bar & Grill

**T**HE best chicken wings in the city, according to wingsnbeer.com (and I concur) can be found at Mug Shotz, a hidden gem at the intersection of Ogden Road and Blackfoot Trail. Over 40 varieties, from mango-chili and raspberry-chipotle to ginger beef and dill pickle, are served up—all in the form of huge, fresh, locally raised wings with lots of meat. (Love the Soy Sensation!)

12, 2808 Ogden Road SE
403.264.4441

## Muku | Japanese Noodles

**M**UKU, the Japanese noodle house run by Globefish, is dedicated to ramen noodles and the broths and toppings that come with it. Broths here are either miso or pork, and toppings can include things like roast pork, boiled eggs, greens, vegetables and sprouts, creating a hot, lightly flavoured bowl of goodness. Muku is great for a fast, reasonably priced, chilly-day lunch.

326 – 14 Street NW
403.283.6555

## Naaco Truck | Neo-Retro Indian

**T**AKE traditional Indian food, shake in a bit of Mexican presentation and you have a "naaco," part nan, part taco. There's spice, there's crunch, there's warm nan bread wrapped around most items, like the butter chicken. The bright colours of the truck and its owners' smiles will brighten your day. Note: The spicy chickpea fritters are always a treat—never greasy, always hot.

Food Truck
No phone

thenaacotruck.com

## Naina's Kitchen | Comfort Food

**N**AINA'S (grandmother in Welsh) breakfasts and lunches are great, but it's her stuffed burgers that really draw out the crowd. They're a half-pound of freshly ground beef stuffed with your choice from a list of cheeses, mushrooms, bacon, pulled pork, and on and on. Great burger, great fries—bring an appetite and napkins. Her selection of eight grilled cheese sandwiches is pretty popular, too.

8, 2808 Ogden Road SE
403.263.6355

nainaskitchen.com

## Nem Delight | Vietnamese

**T**HE tiny Nem Delight (no seats, takeout only) in Deer Ridge serves some of the best Vietnamese food in the city. Run by the former owners of Saigon (my favourite Vietnamese restaurant for years) and their niece Cam Do, a SAIT-trained chef, Nem provides excellent, crispy-hot cha gio (imperial rolls) and bun packed with rice vermicelli, meats, vegetables and lovely seasonings.

13750 Bow Bottom Trail SE
(Deer Valley Station)
403.235.5757

nemdelight.com

## OEB Breakfast

**O**EB breaks over 2,700 fresh, free-run, omega-3 eggs every week. (They have a contract with a local farmer to produce eggs just for OEB.) There are eggs scrambled with lobster and shrimp and topped with a brown butter hollandaise, plus pages of other great eggy breakfasts. Fine coffee, too. And they fry all their potato dishes in organic duck fat. Yum!

824 Edmonton Trail NE
403.278.3447

eatoeb.com

## Papa Chocolat

Chocolatier

**B**ERNARD Callebaut has gone back to his chocolate-making roots with this new shop in Willow Park, and he's also opened a booth at the Simons Valley Ranch market. He combines the finest Belgian chocolate with exotic ingredients to create delicate, artisanal chocolates like his La Mer, milk chocolate with sea salt. Or the Geisha Caffe, milk chocolate ganache infused with Panamanian coffee and cloaked in semi-sweet chocolate.

10816 Macleod Trail S
(Willow Park Village)
403.264.7212

14555 Symons Valley Road NW
(Symons Valley Ranch)
No phone

papachocolat.ca

## Pascal's Patisserie

Take & Bake Pastries

**H**AVE you always wanted your kitchen to smell like a grand French patisserie? Pick up Pascal's frozen, unbaked croissants and pastries from various retail locations (check the website) or from their bakery on 1A Street SE, thaw and proof them overnight, then bake them yourself. Check out their website for cafés and restaurants that carry their baked pastries, too.

101, 5240 – 1A Street SE
403.968.6156

pascals.ca

## Pâtisserie du Soleil | Casual French Bistro

**A**H, a taste of France in Woodbine. Pâtisserie du Soleil bakes French breads, pastries, pies, cakes and squares daily. They also cook beef bourguignon, cassoulet, steak frites and braised lamb shanks (all under $15) to complete the French experience at lunch or dinner. I always enjoy the breakfast scones, and their hot chocolate is a winner. The new Bow outlet has a couple of hot options, plus sandwiches, salads and baked goods.

2525 Woodview Drive SW
(Woodbine Square)
403.452.8833

205, 500 Centre Street S
(The Bow)
403.718.0399

patisseriedusoleil.com

## Pelican Pier | Seafood Café & Market

**T**HE nautically themed, family-friendly Pelican Pier on the shores of 14th Street NW surprises many folks with its simple location. But the lightly battered fish (pollock, haddock, cod, halibut or salmon—your choice!) and chips are superb. I'm a fan of the haddock, and with a bowl of their seafood chowder, I'm ready to set sail. (Note: It's a fine seafood market, too.)

4404 – 14 Street NW
403.289.6100

pelicanpier.ca

## Pies Plus | Pie Café

**D**ECISIONS, decisions. With over 80 pies on the Pies Plus menu, how does one choose? It's something to mull over while lunching on a hearty soup, a sandwich or some chili. Strawberry-peach? Yuleberry? (That's apple, cranberry and strawberry.) Raisin? Pumpkin pecan? Perhaps just start at apple and work your way through the list alphabetically. (And those are good soups, sandwiches and chili, by the way.)

12445 Lake Fraser Drive SE
(Avenida Village)
403.271.6616

piespluscafe.com

## Pimento's | Pizza & Gelato

**P**IMENTO's chef/owner Mario Spina bakes primo pizza flowers and cones in his high-tech Italian machines. Of course, you can also get a flat pizza. Whichever way you choose, his are some of the best pizzas around. Mario makes his own gelato, too, usually about a half-dozen flavours of whatever strikes his fancy at any given time. His Pimento's food truck offers both pizzas and gelato, too.

814 – 1 Avenue NE
403.515.0065

pimentos.ca

## Pio | Peruvian

**P**ERUVIAN fast food—rotisserie chicken laced with high-mountain Peruvian herbs, anticuchos (skewered bits of beef heart), pollo saltado (pan-fried chicken with vegetables and fries) and even ceviche—is on the menu at this family-run restaurant. Try a glass of chicha morada (their lemonade made with Peruvian purple corn) and some alfajores (shortbread cookies sandwiching the sweet dulce de leche) for dessert.

2929 Sunridge Way NE
403.681.7378

pioperu.com

## Prairie Mill | Whole Grain Bakery

**O**RGANIC wheat is milled on-site and the flour is then hand-kneaded into weighty loaves. A dozen types of bread are baked daily, along with banana bread, cinnamon rolls and cookies. The breads (which have no preservatives or oils) are fully natural and great for sandwiches, toast or enjoying on their own. The shop always has samples of bread still warm from the oven.

4820 Northland Drive NW
(Northland Plaza)
403.282.6455

prairiemillbread.com

## Reader's Garden Café

Regional Garden Fare

311 – 25 Avenue SE
403.263.0210

readersgardencafe.ca

**T**HIS seasonal café in the beautiful Reader Rock Garden provides an excellent view of Stampede Park, along with light meals of garden-fresh cuisine. Salads like fresh herbs with baby greens and carrots and entrees like free-range chicken with cream dumplings take us back to the 1920s in this rebuild of William Reader's house. (Reader was Calgary's first Parks Superintendent.) Be sure to take a stroll around the garden.

## Red Tree

Gourmet Market
& Catering

2129 – 33 Avenue SW
403.242.3246

redtreecatering.com

**A**s well as being one of the city's finest caterers, Marda Loop's Red Tree offers fine foods to-go, from an artichoke and chevre mousse with preserved lemon to miso-marinated flank steak with sautéed mushrooms and baby bok choy. Chefs/partners Aaron Creurer and Susan Hopkins and their staff create lovely desserts like pistachio-orange cannoli and strawberry tarts, too.

## Red Wagon Diner

Montreal Smoked Meat

Food Truck
403.991.9696

redwagondiner.com

**T**HE Red Wagon Diner food truck keeps life simple. Their focus is on Montreal smoked meat sandwiches served four different ways, including a Reuben and a basic one with house mustard on rye. There's also a smoked meat hash with sautéed mushrooms, onions, banana peppers, cheese and two soft eggs with rye toast on the side, plus one vegetarian option.

## Rocky's Burgers

### Great Big Burgers

**P**ULL up to the old Calgary Transit bus parked off 12th Street SE and enjoy a great burger. The secret? The hand-formed patty is steamed before it's grilled. Have some finger-scorching fries, too. On a nice day, dine in Rocky's dining room, the prairie grass-covered hillside with a few picnic tables. (But watch out for the gophers—they're devious devils when it comes to fries.)

4645 – 12 Street SE
403.243.0405

rockysburgers.com

## Rustic Sourdough

### German Bakery & Deli

**T**HE deli side of Rustic Sourdough on 17th Avenue serves up thick sandwiches on their always-fresh sourdough bread (choose from 80 cold cuts and 40 cheeses), plus a couple of hearty soups. The bakery side offers classic Swiss-inspired breads, cookies, pastries and cakes (only baked goods are available at the farmers' market locations). There's always something good for dessert here—we had a Rustic Black Forest cake for my parents' 60th anniversary that satisfied every appetite in the family.

1305 – 17 Avenue SW
403.245.2113

7711 Macleod Trail S
(Kingsland Farmers' Market)
No phone

14555 Symons Valley Road NW
(Symons Valley Ranch)
No phone

rusticsourdoughbakery.ca

## Selkirk Grille

### Canadiana

**S**TROLLING Heritage Park's exhibits (I love the new Gasoline Alley) can be appetite-generating business. Where better to stop than at the Selkirk Grille, where panko-crusted crab and shrimp cakes and roasted lamb loin dot a menu of contemporary classics? The big, high-tech kitchen here supplies the rest of Heritage Park with food, too. Note: Hours and menus change seasonally.

1900 Heritage Drive SW
(Heritage Park)
403.268.8607

heritagepark.ca

## Sidewalk Citizen

Artisan Bread,
Bakery, Deli

Aviv Fried and Michal Lavi are building a small baking empire one cheese stick at a time. From their original bakery amid the Manchester muffler shops to their bakery and deli in Sunnyside Market, their breads are crisply crusted, the Danishes are laden with delicious fruit, and the sandwiches and pizzas are truly spectacular. (Look for more goodies in the redeveloped Simmons Building in 2015.)

5524 – 1A Street SW
403.457.2245

10, 338 – 10 Street NW
(Sunnyside Natural Market)
403.460.9065

sidewalkcitizenbakery.com

## Siraia

Modern Classics

Between Siraia and its sister restaurant Ibby's Lounge at the Sirocco golf course, there are good options for either a golf-focused meal or a quick out-of-Calgary getaway. The crab cakes are great, the tuna burger on a brioche bun is outstanding and the shepherd's pie is hearty whether your golf game has failed you or not. The clubhouse also offers a sweeping view from the Prairies to the Rockies.

Sirocco Golf Club
(4 km south of Spruce Meadows on Spruce Meadows Way)
403.201.5505

sirocco.ca

## Soffritto

Oils, Vinegars & Deli

Soffritto would be interesting enough just for its collection of olive oils and balsamic vinegars—they carry fresh oils from all over the world and some mighty tasty infused vinegars. There are always over a couple dozen of each to sample and buy. But what takes Soffritto over the top is the delicious collection of fresh foods to-go, gourmet ingredients and humongous sandwiches made to order.

2116, 380 Canyon Meadows Drive SE
403.278.2728

## Springbank Cheese | Cheese Shop

**W**ITH more than 350 cheeses (400 at Christmastime) lining the coolers at the Willow Park shop, Springbank is a great place to pick up the freshest curds or the stinkiest rind-washed rounds. All your cheesy accessories—crackers, spreads, knives, boards and cheesy advice—are available too. Fine cheeses and accoutrements are also at the 14th Street NW, Marda Loop and Crowfoot locations, with quality always at the forefront.

10816 Macleod Trail S
(Willow Park Village)
403.225.6040

Check website for
3 more locations

springbankcheese.ca

## Stromboli Inn | Pizza

**I**N the 1970s and 1980s, Stromboli Inn was a hot spot for hand-tossed pizza made with twice-proofed dough. Thick but tasty, Stromboli pizza had a unique flavour and texture. The family-run operation was in hiatus for years, but resurfaced in 2013 in this small Bridgeland location. Now under the able hands of Peter Tudda, son of the original owners, it's back and as good as ever.

614 – 1 Avenue NE
403.265.8680

## Sunnyside Natural Market | Natural Market

**F**OCUSING on local and organic whenever possible, Sunnyside Market provides a huge range of recycled (and recyclable) goods, including paper and cleaning products, in addition to their excellent produce, meats, dairy products and other grocery wares. An expansion and inclusion of a Sidewalk Citizen bakery and deli in 2013 has increased their already large customer base.

10, 338 – 10 Street NW
403.270.7474

sunnysidemarket.ca

## Sweetgrass Deli

**R**OLAND Griesser, formerly of Canmore's Railway Deli, has opened shop in Okotoks with Sweetgrass Deli. From Monday through Saturday, Sweetgrass whips up eggy breakfasts and fresh lunches of soups and sandwiches at reasonable prices. There are always fruit pies, carrot cake and croissants fresh from the oven, too. (And turduckens for Thanksgiving and Christmas.)

### Deli

1, 49 Elizabeth Street
Okotoks
403.995.4454

sweetgrassdeli.com

## Thai It Up

**T**HAI It Up has a short list of lunch and dinner Thai dishes (plus an Indian one or two), but whether at their Canmore café or their Chameleon food truck, this is lovely food. Chef/owner Kevin Bellis knows his pad Thai from his som tam salad and packs them with a hearty punch of chilies. Don't miss his banh mi baguette sandwiches or his butter chicken poutine.

### Thai

731 Railway Avenue
Canmore
403.675.8424

thaiitup.ca

## Tropical Delight

**T**HE big draw at Tropical Delight is laksa, a hearty Malaysian lunch soup. Laksa has a coconut milk and fish- or chicken-stock base, piqued by chilies and filled with meats or seafoods, some vegetables and a big swirl of noodles. Tropical Delight's laksa is made with shrimp, sea legs and fish balls and has layers and layers of flavour. (It brings the heat, too.)

### Malaysian

4604 – 12 Street NE
403.261.1811

## Valbella Café | European Deli

**T**HE lengthy list of meats that Valbella produces is a carnivores dream: 14 preparations of bacon, 16 of ham, 17 of chicken and turkey, and 20 of air-dried meats. (Mmmm . . . air-dried meats.) You can buy them to devour on the way home or dine in at the deli. Or both. Valbella has racks of appropriately meaty condiments and dry goods, too.

104 Elk Run Boulevard
Canmore
403.678.9989

valbellagourmetfoods.ca

## Vendome | Bistro Café

**V**ENDOME is a rustic, creaky-floored, energetic, all-ages joint that serves locally roasted Paradise Mountain coffee and whips up duck confit and truffle aioli sandwiches, salted caramel French toast with caramelized bananas, and three versions of eggs Benedict. I like the one with the house-cured gravlax, capers and cream cheese, a fine way to while away a morning in Sunnyside.

940 – 2 Avenue NW
403.453.1140

vendomecafe.com

 ## Village Ice Cream | Ice Cream

**H**AND-CRAFTED ice cream in a fresh-rolled waffle cone. What's not to like? At Village Ice Cream, the lineup can be long, but the wait, uber-creamy and rewarding. Maple pecan, toasted coconut and huckleberry are favourites, but watch for creative seasonal flavours—maybe toasted marshmallow will be your new fave. Mine is the rum raisin. Catherine's is the chili-chocolate.

431 – 10 Avenue SE
403.261.7950

villageicecream.com

## White Gold
Artisan Cheese Factory

**F**RESH fior di latte cheese is made daily in the traditional style of Bojano, Italy at White Gold. It's fresh, it's light and it now adorns many local Caprese salads, pizzas and other fine restaurant dishes. Go to the source to purchase hand-crafted cheeses and make your own meals sing (in Italian, that is). Aged cheese such as caciocavallo and provolone are also available and are excellent.

6, 1319 – 45 Avenue NE
403.402.2031

fiordilatte.ca

## Wilde Grainz
Artisan Bakery

**S**KILFUL artisanal baking comes out of Inglewood's Wilde Grainz under the talented hands of Teddi Smith and Karen Schoenrank. Croissants take on a new life, breads are elevated to "I don't even need butter" status, and cakes are almost too elegant to eat. Even a simple cookie here is a thing of beauty. They carry gluten-free options, too. Just go.

1218 – 9 Avenue SE
403.767.9006

## Yann Haute Patisserie
Patisserie

**T**HIS is the place for macarons, from blackcurrant and violet to orange blossom and Grand Marnier to peanut butter and jelly. Yann Blanchard is a master of the baking arts and prepares a daily menu of breads, pastries and cakes to go along with over two dozen flavours of macarons. You can even have a macaron cake or a tower of macarons built on a chocolate cone. (Too much? *Jamais!*)

329 – 23 Avenue SW
403.244.8091

yannboutique.com

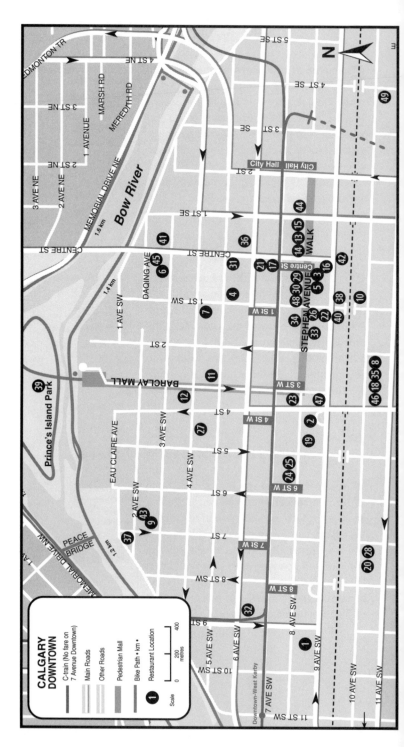

# Dining in Downtown Calgary (Legend)

1. Atlas
2. Belgo
3. Belvedere, The
4. Black Betty (LE)
5. Blink
6. Bliss & Co. (LE)
7. Bliss & Co. (LE)
8. Briggs
9. Buchanan's
10. Buzzards
11. Caffè Artigiano (see CT)
12. Caffè Artigiano (see CT)

13. Caffe Rosso (see CT)
14. Catch
15. Centini
16. Charcut
17. Colonial
18. Craft Beer Market (LE)
19. Cucina
20. Decadent Desserts (LE)
21. DeVille (see CT)
22. DeVille (see CT)
23. Double Zero
24. Downtownfood

25. Escoba
26. Falafel King (LE)
27. Glory of India
28. Holy Grill (LE)
29. Home
30. James Joyce (LE)
31. Jelly Modern (LE)
32. Jonas' Restaurant
33. Libertine, The
34. Mango Shiva
35. National Beer Hall
36. Pâtisserie du Soleil (LE)

37. Q
38. Rimrock, The
39. River Café
40. Rush
41. Silver Dragon
42. Sky 360
43. Spice 7
44. Teatro
45. Thai Bistro
46. Thai Sa-on
47. TotaliTea (see CT)
48. Trib
49. Village Ice Cream (LE)

(LE) indicates entry is in "Little Eats" section on pages 143 – 171

(see CT) indicates entry is mentioned in the introduction to the "Coffee (and Tea, too)" section on page 174

 downtown calgary

Foodies unite with the unique culinary offerings located in Downtown Calgary. Grand rooms showcase fine dining, cutting-edge bistros serve up the latest in food and wine, and tasty ethnic spots bring the world to Calgary. Another palatable perk is reduced rates for evening and weekend parking. **www.downtowncalgary.com**

# Coffee (and Tea, too)

**W**E love our caffeinated beverages. Calgary has become a global leader in all things coffee, and tea shops are becoming more popular, too. Below are some of my favourites outside of the downtown core. A number of them have some pretty good food, too.

For a few more primo cups, try Bluerock (Okotoks), Caffe Crema, Central Blends, Home Ground (Okotoks), Java Jamboree (Cochrane), the Naked Leaf, Oolong Tea House and Purple Perk.

And don't forget, downtown Calgary hosts a number of tasty spots, too: Caffè Artigiano, Caffe Rosso, DeVille and TotaliTea. See them on the map on page 172. (Note: Caffe Rosso, DeVille and TotaliTea also have outlets outside of downtown.)

## Beamer's

**T**HE essential starting point for any Canmore hiking or skiing venture, Beamer's fuels you with caffeine and a fine side of muffins, cookies or breakfast treats. Good for sedentary visitors, too.

737–7 Avenue
Canmore
403.609.0111

1702 Bow Valley Trail
Canmore
403.678.3988

beamerscoffeebar.ca

## Bumpy's

**F**ROM the fresh-baked muffins and quiche to the lasagna and grilled panini, Bumpy's offers a palate-pleasing, home-style feed plus excellent espresso drinks and top-notch personalized service.

1040 – 8 Street SW
403.265.0244

bumpyscafe.com

## Cadence

**C**ADENCE calls itself a 21st Century Diner and has a list of breakfast items and lunch sandwiches to back up their coffee. Non-Bownesians welcome.

6407 Bowness Road NW
403.247.9955

cadencecoffee.com

## Caffè Beano

**B**EANO has been the de facto 17th Avenue community centre since 1990. Fratello coffee beans enliven the action, especially with an outstanding molasses muffin.

1613 – 9 Street SW
403.229.1232

caffebeano.ca

## Communitea

**G**REAT coffee and tea house, live entertainment centre, breakfast and lunch meet-up joint (with gluten-free and vegan options), kid-friendly café and all-round green business. That's Communitea.

117, 1001 – 6 Avenue
Canmore
403.678.6818

thecommunitea.com

## Espresso Pi Café

**D**RAWING on the name of their darkest espresso, Big Mountain Coffee Roasters has opened their own coffee shop in Crossroads Market. They pull lush espressos through a La Spaziale S40 machine.

1235 – 26 Avenue SE
(Crossroads Market)
403.244.6864

bigmountaincoffeeroasters.ca

## Fratello Analog

**F**RATELLO has roasted beans for eons. Now they're building espresso machines for many coffee houses in our area and beyond. And, they've opened a couple of their own shops to show off their goods. The 17th Avenue shop is simply called Analog.

510 – 77 Avenue SE
(Calgary Farmers' Market)
No phone

740 – 17 Avenue SW
No phone

fratellocoffee.com

## Gravity

**G**RAVITY reaches beyond their primo espresso fare with a couple dozen carefully selected wines and beers plus good breakfasts, lunches and desserts. Check out the Balti curry nights on Friday and Saturday.

909 – 10 Street SE
(Atlantic Avenue Art Block)
403.457.0697

cafegravity.com

## Kawa

**K**AWA uses 49th Parallel, Elysian, Josuma and Intelligentsia beans to create excellent coffee. The café appeals to a broad market with its tasty sandwiches, empanadas, b'stilla pies, and great beer and wine list.

101, 1333 – 8 Street SW
403.452.5233

kawacalgary.ca

## Phil & Sebastian

**S**TARTING with a small farmers' market booth, two young engineers have built a serious coffee empire that has them roasting and shipping their beans across Canada. Soups and sandwiches, plus baked goods, round out the menu in the Marda Loop and Chinook Centre locations.

2043 – 33 Avenue SW
403.686.1221

6455 Macleod Trail S
(Chinook Centre)
403.255.4900

14555 Symons Valley Road NW
(Symons Valley Ranch)
No phone

philsebastian.com

## The Roasterie

**T**HE oldest coffee roasterie in the city keeps on doing its thing, roasting and pulling shots for a fascinating band of regulars who've been coming for decades.

314 – 10 Street NW
403.270.3304

## Savour

**A** FRATELLO Slayer machine sits atop Savour's counter at this new, 30-seat coffee house in Mission. Nice digs and friendly staff. A few sweets and Vietnamese subs round out the menu.

21, 2500 – 4 Street SW
587.353.5370

# The Lists

THESE lists will guide you to various food styles, geographic areas and special picks. Entries are in alphabetical order in the "Big Eats" section of the book unless one of the following notations is behind the name of the establishment: **LE**, which means an entry is in alphabetical order in the "Little Eats" section; **CT**, which means it's in the "Coffee (and Tea, too)" section; *see* **CT**, which means it's mentioned in the introduction to the "Coffee (and Tea, too)" section.

## Northeast Calgary

Big Fish
Boccavino
Boogie's (LE)
Bridgeland Market (LE)
Carino
Clay Oven
Delhi Darbar
DeVille (*see* CT)
El Charrito (LE)
Fiasco Gelato (LE)
Holy Smoke (LE)
Il Sogno
Inti
Lina's (LE)
Namskar
Nirvana
OEB Breakfast (LE)
Open Range
Pimento's (LE)
Pio (LE)
Rea's
Santorini
Shigatsu
Shiki (*see* Shikiji)
Shiraz
Silver Inn
Stromboli Inn (LE)
Thai Boat
Tropical Delight (LE)
White Elephant
White Gold (LE)
Zipang

## Northwest Calgary

Blue Door (LE)
Brasserie Kensington
Cadence (CT)
Central Blends (*see* CT)
Chef's Table
Da Guido
Flavours (LE)
4th Spot
Globefish
Juree's
Kaffir Lime (LE)
Kinjo
Marathon

Menyatai (LE)
Muku (LE)
Muse
Naked Leaf, The (*see* CT)
Notable
Oolong Tea House (*see* CT)
Papa Chocolat (LE)
Pelican Pier (LE)
Phil & Sebastian (CT)
Prairie Mill (LE)
Pulcinella
Roasterie, The (CT)
Rustic Sourdough (LE)
Sidewalk Citizen (LE)
Springbank Cheese (LE)
Sultan's Tent
Sushi Club
Szechuan Restaurant
Vendome (LE)
Vero
Wa's

## Southeast Calgary

Alloy
Better Butcher, The (LE)
Big Rock Grill
Blu (LE)
Caffe Rosso (*see* CT)
Calgary Farmers' Market (LE)
Colonial
Crossroads Market (LE)
Espresso Pi Café (CT)
Fine Diner
Fratello Analog (CT)
Gravity (CT)
Holy Smoke (LE)
Jelly Modern (LE)
Knifewear (LE)
Mimo
Mug Shotz (LE)
Naina's (LE)
Nem Delight (LE)
Papa Chocolat (LE)
Pascal's Patisserie (LE)
Pies Plus (LE)
Reader's Garden Café (LE)
Rocky's Burgers (LE)
Rouge

Safari Grill
Soffritto (LE)
Spolumbo's
Springbank Cheese (LE)
Sugo
TotaliTea (*see* CT)
Wellington's
Wilde Grainz (LE)
Without Papers

## Southwest Calgary
Bistro Rouge
Blue Door (LE)
Caffe Crema (*see* CT)
Cassis Bistro
De Thai
Gaucho
Globefish
Himalayan, The
Il Centro
Kaffir Lime (LE)
Kingsland Farmers' Market (LE)
Kinjo
Ladybug, A (LE)
Le Villa
Leo Fu's
Market 17 (LE)
Mercato
Moti Mahal
Pâtisserie du Soleil (LE)
Pfanntastic Pannenkoek
Phil & Sebastian (CT)
Ratatouille
Red Tree (LE)
Rustic Sourdough (LE)
Selkirk Grille (LE)
Sidewalk Citizen (LE)
Springbank Cheese (LE)
Thai Nongkhai
Vin Room

## Beltline/Victoria Park
Avec Bistro
Bonterra
Boxwood
Brix and Morsel (LE)
Bumpy's (CT)
Caffe Rosso (*see* CT)
Casbah, The
Chocolatier
    Bernard Callebaut (LE)
Cookbook Co. Cooks (LE)
Craft Beer Market (LE)
Flatlands
Gaga Pizza (LE)
Grumans
Jelly Modern (LE)
Kawa (CT)
Kickers (LE)

Laurier Lounge
L'Epicerie (LE)
Manuel Latruwe (LE)
Mirchi (*see* Spice 7)
Montagu's (LE)
National Beer Hall
Posto (*see* Bonterra)
Raw Bar
Taste
Village Ice Cream (LE)
Xocolat

## Downtown Calgary
*See pp. 172 – 173*

## Mission/17th Avenue SW
Aida's
Analog (*see* Fratello Analog, CT)
Bar C
Bistro 2210
Blondes
Borgo
Brava Bistro
Caffè Beano (CT)
Candela
Cibo
Clive Burger (LE)
Coup, The
CRMR at Home (LE)
Epiphanie Chocolate (LE)
Farm
Fleur de Sel
Itza Bakeshop (LE)
Janice Beaton Fine Cheese (LE)
Khao San
Koob (LE)
Kuzina
La Boulangerie (LE)
La Chaumière
Le Villa
Living Room, The
Los Chilitos (LE)
Market
Mercato
Model Milk
Ox and Angela
Purple Perk (*see* CT)
Rustic Sourdough (LE)
Sabroso
Savour (CT)
Thai Bistro
Una
Vin Room
Yann Haute Patisserie (LE)

## Banff/Lake Louise
Banffshire Club, The
Barpa Bill's (LE)
Coyotes
Eddie, The (LE)

Laggan's (LE)
Post Hotel
Silver Dragon
Sleeping Buffalo
Three Ravens

## Canmore

Aroma
Beamer's (CT)
Chez François
Clubhouse at Stewart Creek,
    The (LE)
Communitea (CT)
Crazyweed
Gaucho
Junction, The
    (Dead Man's Flats, LE)
O Bistro
Sage Bistro
Thai It Up (LE)
Trough, The
Valbella Café (LE)

## Foothills/Beyond

Bavarian Inn, The (Bragg Creek)
Bistro Provence (Okotoks)
Bluerock (Okotoks, see CT)
Broxburn Café (Lethbridge)
Heartland Café (Okotoks, LE)
Home Ground (Okotoks, see CT)
Jaipur (Cochrane)
Java Jamboree (Cochrane, see CT)
Las Maracas (Okotoks, LE)
Little New York (Longview)
Longview Steakhouse (Longview)
Mehtab (Cochrane)
Siraia (MD of Foothills, LE)
Sweetgrass Deli (Okotoks, LE)
Thai Onzon (Cochrane)

## Baked Goods/Sweets

Bambino by Fiasco
    (see Fiasco Gelato, LE)
Bliss & Co. (LE)
Chocolatier
    Bernard Callebaut (LE)
Decadent Desserts (LE)
Epiphanie Chocolate (LE)
Fiasco Gelato (LE)
Flatlands
Itza Bakeshop (LE)
Jelly Modern (LE)
La Boulangerie (LE)
Ladybug, A (LE)
Laggan's (LE)
Manuel Latruwe (LE)
Papa Chocolat (LE)
Pascal's Patisserie (LE)
Pâtisserie du Soleil (LE)
Pies Plus (LE)

Prairie Mill (LE)
Rustic Sourdough (LE)
Sidewalk Citizen (LE)
Village Ice Cream (LE)
Wilde Grainz (LE)
Yann Haute Patisserie (LE)

## Breakfast/Brunch

Aroma
Bar C
Belgo
Big Fish
Bistro Rouge
Bistro 2210
Borgo
Brasserie Kensington
Bumpy's (CT)
Cadence (CT)
Chef's Table
Chez François
Clubhouse at Stewart Creek,
    The (LE)
Coyotes
Cucina
DeVille (see CT)
Fine Diner
Flatlands
Grumans
Laggan's (LE)
Laurier Lounge
Little New York
Mango Shiva
Manuel Latruwe (LE)
Notable
O Bistro
OEB Breakfast (LE)
Pâtisserie du Soleil (LE)
Pfanntastic Pannenkoek
Post Hotel
Rimrock, The
River Café
Sage Bistro
Silver Dragon
Sky 360
Sleeping Buffalo
Sweetgrass Deli (LE)
Vendome (LE)
Vero
Yellow Door

## Canadian

Banffshire Club, The
Boxwood
Brix and Morsel (LE)
Broxburn Café
Clubhouse at Stewart Creek,
    The (LE)
Downtownfood
Escoba
Farm

Fine Diner
Flatlands
4th Spot
Grumans
Heartland (LE)
Home
Laurier Lounge
Living Room, The
Market
Model Milk
Notable
Open Range
Reader's Garden Café (LE)
Rimrock, The
River Café
Rouge
Sage Bistro
Selkirk Grille (LE)
Siraia (LE)
Sky 360
Sleeping Buffalo

## Chinese

Leo Fu's
Silver Dragon
Silver Inn
Szechuan Restaurant

## Coffee/Tea

*See pp. 174 – 176*

## Contemporary

Alloy
Anju
Bar C
Belvedere, The
Brava Bistro
Carino
Charcut
Chef's Table
Colonial
Coup, The
Crazyweed
Cucina
Downtownfood
Home
Mango Shiva
Market
Model Milk
Muse
O Bistro
Ox and Angela
Raw Bar
River Café
Rouge
Rush
Taste
Three Ravens
Trough, The

Vero
Vin Room

## Diners

Blondes
Cadence (CT)
Fine Diner

## Food Trucks

Bambino by Fiasco
    (*see* Fiasco Gelato, LE)
Braizen (LE)
Chameleon (*see* Thai It Up, LE)
Fiasco Gelato (LE)
Holy Smoke (LE)
Jelly Modern (LE)
JoJo's BBQ (LE)
Naaco Truck (LE)
Pimento's (LE)
Red Wagon Diner (LE)
Rocky's Burgers (LE)
SteakOut Truck (*see* Holy Grill, LE)
Without Papers

## French/Continental

Avec Bistro
Belgo
Big Rock Grill
Bistro Provence
Bistro Rouge
Bistro 2210
Brasserie Kensington
Cassis Bistro
Chef's Table
Chez François
Fleur de Sel
La Boulangerie (LE)
La Chaumière
Ladybug, A (LE)
Laurier Lounge
L'Epicerie (LE)
Post Hotel
Q
Ratatouille

## German/Swiss

Bavarian Inn, The
Rustic Sourdough (LE)
Valbella Café (LE)

## Greek

Barpa Bill's (LE)
Kuzina
Santorini

## Hamburgers

Bistro 2210
Black Betty (LE)
Boogie's (LE)
Buchanan's

Carino
Charcut
Clive Burger (LE)
Eddie, The (LE)
Holy Grill (LE)
Longview Steakhouse
Model Milk
Naina's (LE)
National Beer Hall
Rocky's Burgers (LE)
Siraia (LE)

## Historic Setting

Banffshire, The
Belvedere, The
Bistro Provence
Blink
Bonterra
Boxwood
Catch
Cibo
Home
Il Sogno
James Joyce (LE)
Laurier Lounge
Mango Shiva
Model Milk
Reader's Garden Café (LE)
Rimrock, The
Rouge
Selkirk Grille (LE)
Teatro
Trib
Vendome

## Indian/Pakistani

Clay Oven
Delhi Darbar
Glory of India
Gravity (CT)
Jaipur
Junction, The (LE)
Mango Shiva
Mehtab
Mirchi (*see* Spice 7)
Moti Mahal
Naaco Truck (LE)
Namskar
Nirvana
Safari Grill
Spice 7

## Interesting Ambience

Alloy
Big Fish
Bonterra
Boxwood
Briggs
Broxburn Café
Casbah, The

Double Zero
Farm
Fleur de Sel
Gaucho
Il Centro
Jaipur
Junction, The (LE)
Juree's
Khao San
Kinjo
Le Villa
Longview Steakhouse
Open Range
Raw Bar
River Café
Rush
Santorini
Silver Dragon
Spice 7
Sultan's Tent
Trough, The
Vero
White Elephant
Xocolat

## Italian/Pizza

Boccavino
Bonterra
Borgo
Carino
Centini
Cibo
Cucina
Da Guido
Double Zero
Gaga Pizza (LE)
Il Centro
Il Sogno
Lina's (LE)
Mercato
Pimento's (LE)
Posto (*see* Bonterra)
Pulcinella
Rea's
Sidewalk Citizen (LE)
Spolumbo's
Stromboli Inn (LE)
Sugo
Teatro
Una
Without Papers

## Japanese/Sushi

Carino
Globefish
Kinjo
Menyatai (LE)
Muku (LE)
Shigatsu
Shiki (*see* Shikiji)

Shikiji
Sushi Club
Wa's
Zipang

## Latin American

Aroma
Candela
El Charrito (LE)
Gaucho
Inti
Las Maracas (LE)
Los Chilitos (LE)
Pio (LE)
Sabroso
Xocolat

## Markets

Atlas
Better Butcher, The (LE)
Blu (LE)
Blue Door (LE)
Calgary Farmers' Market (LE)
Cookbook Co. Cooks (LE)
CRMR at Home (LE)
Crossroads Market (LE)
El Charrito (LE)
Janice Beaton Fine Cheese (LE)
Kingsland Farmers' Market (LE)
L'Epicerie (LE)
Lina's (LE)
Market 17 (LE)
Mercato
Red Tree (LE)
Soffritto (LE)
Springbank Cheese (LE)
Sweetgrass Deli (LE)
Symons Valley Ranch
    (see Blue Door, LE; Kaffir
    Lime, LE; Papa Chocolat, LE;
    Phil & Sebastian, CT; Rustic
    Sourdough, LE)
White Gold (LE)

## Meaty

Atlas
Bavarian Inn, The
Better Butcher, The (LE)
Black Betty (LE)
Braizen (LE)
Briggs
Buchanan's
Charcut
Eddie, The (LE)
Gaucho
Holy Smoke (LE)
Inti
JoJo's BBQ (LE)
Kickers (LE)
Koob (LE)

Le Villa
Libertine, The
Longview Steakhouse
Open Range
Red Wagon Diner (LE)
Rocky's Burgers (LE)
Rush
Santorini
Shiraz
Silver Inn
Spolumbo's
SteakOut Truck (see Holy Grill, LE)
Trib
Valbella Café (LE)
Wellington's

## Middle Eastern/Persian

Aida's
Atlas
Falafel King
Koob
Shiraz

## Most Obscure

Atlas
Clay Oven
Double Zero
Downtownfood
Himalayan, The
Inti
Jonas' Restaurant
Mimo
Pfanntastic Pannenkoek
Spice 7
Village Ice Cream (LE)
Wa's
White Elephant

## One of a Kind (Almost)

Anju (Modern Korean)
Coyotes (Southwestern)
Flavours (Nigerian, LE)
Grumans (Jewish-Inspired Deli)
Himalayan, The (Nepalese)
Jonas' Restaurant (Hungarian)
Kaffir Lime (Indonesian, LE)
Knifewear (Knives, LE)
Marathon (Ethiopian)
Montagu's (Sandwiches, LE)
Mug Shotz (Wings, LE)
Pfanntastic Pannenkoek
    (Dutch Pancakes)
Red Tree (Catering, LE)
Tropical Delight (Malaysian, LE)

## Pubs

Buzzards
Craft Beer Market (LE)
James Joyce (LE)
Libertine, The

Mug Shotz (LE)
National Beer Hall

## Romantic

Alloy
Bonterra
Candela
Casbah, The
Laurier Lounge
Rimrock, The
River Café
Sultan's Tent

## Seafood

Big Fish
Blu (LE)
Catch
Mimo
Pelican Pier (LE)
Raw Bar

## Tapas

Brix and Morsel (LE)
Candela
Cibo
Home
Muse
Ox and Angela
Taste
Vin Room

## Thai

Chameleon (*see* Thai It Up, LE)
De Thai
Juree's
Khao San
Thai Bistro
Thai Boat
Thai It Up (LE)
Thai Nongkhai
Thai Onzon
Thai Sa-on
White Elephant

## Vegetarian

Aida's
Broxburn Café
Communitea (CT)
Coup, The
Falafel King (LE)
Heaven (LE)
Marathon
Thai Onzon

## Vietnamese

Colonial
Nem Delight (LE)

## Western Mediterranean

Candela
Casbah, The
Little New York
Ox and Angela
Ratatouille
Sultan's Tent
Una

## Best Bang for Your Buck

Aida's
Atlas
Barpa Bill's
Flatlands
4th Spot
Inti
Jonas' Restaurant
Juree's
Nem Delight (LE)
Pelican Pier (LE)
Rocky's Burgers (LE)
Szechuan Restaurant

## Best Booze

Alloy
Avec Bistro
Bar C
Belgo
Belvedere, The
Big Rock Grill
Blink
Bonterra
Boxwood
Brava Bistro
Buchanan's
Buzzards
Candela
Charcut
Craft Beer Market (LE)
De Thai
James Joyce (LE)
Kawa (LE)
La Chaumière
Living Room, The
Market
Model Milk
National Beer Hall
Ox and Angela
Post Hotel
Raw Bar
River Café
Rouge
Rush
Sage Bistro
Taste
Teatro
Thai Nongkhai
Thai Sa-on
Una
Vin Room

## Best Business Lunch
*If someone else is paying:*

Alloy
Avec Bistro
Belvedere, The
Blink
Buchanan's
Catch
Centini
Home
Il Sogno
La Chaumière
Rimrock, The
River Café
Rouge
Teatro
Wellington's

## Best Business Lunch
*If you are paying:*

Big Rock Grill
Bistro 2210
Bonterra
Centini
Charcut
Clay Oven
Downtownfood
Escoba
Flatlands
Grumans
La Chaumière
Libertine, The
Q
Rustic Sourdough
Spolumbo's
Yellow Door

## Best Patios/Decks

Alloy
Bar C
Bavarian Inn, The
Bonterra
Boxwood
Buzzards
Chef's Table
Cibo
La Chaumière
Laurier Lounge
Living Room, The
Raw Bar
River Café
Rouge
Sage Bistro
Siraia (LE)
Vin Room

## Best Service

Avec Bistro
Belvedere, The
Bistro Rouge
Blink
Bonterra
Brava Bistro
Cassis Bistro
Da Guido
De Thai
Fleur de Sel
Il Sogno
Jonas' Restaurant
La Chaumière
Muse
Post Hotel
Q
River Café
Rouge
Rush
Santorini
Sugo
Sultan's Tent
Teatro
Thai Onzon
Vero
Wellington's

## Best View

Boxwood
Brasserie Kensington
Crazyweed
Post Hotel
Q
Reader's Garden Café (LE)
River Café
Sage Bistro
Siraia (LE)
Sky 360
Sleeping Buffalo
Three Ravens

## Best Washrooms

Belvedere, The
Borgo
Candela
Centini
Cibo
Fleur de Sel
National Beer Hall
Rush